about
Caron Mil......

JUGGLING the demands of a successful career, a thriving company, the lives of three busy children and a bulging shopping trolley is all in a day's work for enterprising businesswoman Caron Milham.

Author of the best-selling *Australian Healthy Shopping Guide* (2007), Caron is an accredited practising dietitian (APD) with more than 25 years' experience in the areas of nutrition and weight loss. Her extensive knowledge of fitness and weight management stem not only from this experience but also from an earlier career as a fitness instructor and competitor in the National Aerobics Championships.

Caron now runs her own health and weight management company and has created the successful *chOOz to lOOz®* program in response to her clients' weight-loss needs.

She has been a guest lecturer at Flinders University, South Australia, has worked as a consultant for government authorities, including the Department of Health, and continues to advise businesses, sporting teams and individuals in her area of expertise.

Caron regularly provides advice on talkback radio, in magazines and has made many appearances on national TV programs including *Today Tonight, A Current Affair, Channel Ten News* and *Channel Seven News*. She is also a supportive mentor to other APDs.

A passionate advocate of the benefits of a healthy lifestyle, Caron believes her mission is to offer practical solutions for permanent weight loss and to inspire others to strive for good health and enjoyment throughout their lives.

AUSTRALIAN

Healthy Cooking Guide

Caron Milham

RANDOM HOUSE AUSTRALIA

foreword

The *Australian Healthy Cooking Guide* is the ideal partner to the *Australian Healthy Shopping Guide*, also written by Caron Milham. It provides a logical sequel by incorporating healthy cooking and a healthy eating plan that outlines meal size, variety and frequency, and that will satisfy even the most fastidious palate.

It covers all food groups, and kids and vegetarians are not forgotten.

Each recipe is garnished with a nutritional contents panel to further aid appropriate selection for those who are aware they have specific nutritional problems.

Nibbles, cakes and between-meal snacks are provided to help the less committed weight loss candidate.

Overall, Caron simplifies the nutritional steps for a healthier lifestyle, namely:

1 Shop sensibly
2 Cook carefully
3 Eat educationally

If we follow these books and their timely advice, along with the judicious use of exercise, not only will we live longer but we will also have a better quality of life and, hopefully, in time eliminate 'diabesity' from the Australian landscape.

David B Bowman FRACP
Gastroenterologist

contents

1

Healthy
Start

2
Healthy Cook

3
Healthy Plan

welcome

Do you often wish that you and your family could have a long and healthy life? Do you dream of staying slim by eating wholesome, delicious and easy-to-prepare meals? Do you yearn for more hours in the day and wish you had more energy to maintain a good balance in your life?

We can't live forever but we can live longer and love what we eat!

It helps to know and understand food – where it comes from, how to prepare and cook it and which ingredients go best together.

THE *Australian Healthy Cooking Guide* shows you how, by taking the hard work and guesswork out of cooking and preparing great food.

I have seen lifestyles change dramatically in my 25 years as a dietitian. In a world full of push-button technology, drive-through takeaways and home-delivered meals, we tend to work more, exercise less and rely on short cuts. Many more people are overweight, and they seem to be achieving this at an earlier age. Our knowlege of healthy food preparation varies greatly – some of my clients can't boil an egg while others are gourmet chefs.

Fortunately, there are ways to enjoy delicious short cuts with food without sacrificing health and flavour.

I have written the *Australian Healthy Cooking Guide* to help those of you who want to be healthy, lose weight or have to deal with medical conditions such as high blood pressure, diabetes or elevated blood cholesterol.

I am proud that the book I self-published in March 2007, the *Australian Healthy Shopping Guide*, became a bestseller within four weeks of its release.

Now I offer the *Australian Healthy Cooking Guide*. Together, these books are the perfect partners to guide you through the purchasing of healthy Australian brands and the planning of delicious and nutritious meals the whole family will enjoy.

Inside the *Australian Healthy Cooking Guide* you'll find:

○ Healthy meal ideas for those on low-fat (saturated and trans fat), low-sugar, low-salt, diabetic, weight-loss, vegetarian and high-fibre diets

○ Symbols showing recipes that can be adapted for different health conditions (*see page 43*)

○ Nutritional breakdown of recipes using the latest Foodworks 2007 technology, giving a nutrient analysis in kilojoules, calories, fat, saturated fat, protein, carbohydrate, fibre and sodium (salt) per serve

○ Comprehensive menu plans spanning two weeks, as well as shopping lists that make it quick and easy to get everything you need in one go

○ Hundreds of timesaving, healthy and tasty food tips using around three easy-to-find and affordable ingredients

○ More than 120 quick and easy recipes, from everyday basics to healthier versions of old favourites

○ Impressive gourmet recipes for meals that taste delicious but don't take much time or money

○ Beginners hints that provide basic cooking tips, such as poaching the perfect egg

○ Vegetarian and children's recipes that everyone will enjoy

○ The perfect companion to the *Australian Healthy Shopping Guide* (*AHSG*)

choose health

There are many delicious and practical food short cuts that don't involve sacrificing health and taste. The *AHCG* shows you where to start, what to cook and how to plan for a healthy outcome.

Got it covered
The *Australian Healthy Cooking Guide* (*AHCG*) is packed with handy hints, recipe variations, diet tips and healthy lifestyle suggestions. If you need further explanation of medical or nutritional terminology, refer to the Resources section on page 185. For more detailed information, and particularly if you have health concerns, contact an accredited practising dietitian or your GP.

1 Healthy Start

This section presents essential food facts, tried-and-tested preparation tips and clever cooking hints to get you started on the road to healthy eating fast! If you are short on time or need some inspiration, you'll learn what you should aim for, what you should limit, how to plan effectively and how to create healthy alternatives – all this while still avoiding the weekly kilojoule blowout. There are useful ideas for stocking your pantry, fridge and freezer efficiently and a comprehensive list of essential kitchen equipment.

2 Healthy Cook

You'll be introduced to delicious new recipes as well as practical guidelines to help you adapt some of your old favourites. All recipes and tips in this section and throughout the *AHCG* are suitable for those of you with diabetes, high blood cholesterol, high blood pressure or those wishing to lose weight, unless otherwise indicated with a symbol (*see page 43*). You can still include the recipes carrying a symbol as long as you make the suggested modifications with some ingredients.

> It's not just the mouthfuls in your life, but the life in your mouthfuls.

Australia has a wonderful variety of fresh, tasty and affordable food. Experiment and take advantage of it.

3 Healthy Plan

Here you'll find detailed menu-planning guidelines specifically for weight loss and weight control, timesaving shopping lists to make it easy to find what you want in the supermarket and two weeks of sample menus using recipes from the book, all conveniently page-referenced. There's expert advice on tailoring and varying the menu plans to give you as much structure or flexibility as you need. There are also tips on boosting motivation as well as practical ways to steer clear of temptation.

chOOz TO lOOz®

■ chOOz to lOOz is a weight-loss and management program that I developed to help clients achieve permanent weight control. The program focuses on the mechanics of weight loss, the psychological basis of eating habits and health management, and motivational techniques. It uses practical, balanced, satisfying and easy-to-follow menu plans that can be personalised to suit clients' needs.

■ The chOOz to lOOz program uses **exchanges** to help maintain variety in its menu plans. **Exchanges** are food items that belong to different food groups but are of similar nutrient value. In Part 3, *Healthy Plan*, you can tailor and vary your menu plan using the exchange list, which gives daily and weekly alternatives.

1

Healthy
Start

get organised

Many of us feel daunted by the prospect of preparing healthy meals because we think it will be time-consuming. The key to kitchen success is organisation – use your time well and plan ahead. It helps relieve the post-work stress too! Stay motivated by making food an adventure and try new foods every week.

Be a chef in the kitchen but not a slave to it!

Visit the markets to explore the different stalls and the vast array of fresh produce available.

PLANNING your menus, meals, cooking times, shopping expeditions and lists ahead of time or for at least two days a week helps you save time, energy and money, not to mention petrol, electricity and stress.

Use the menu-planning guidelines and ideas in Part 3, *Healthy Plan* (page 164). These contain a two-week menu plan and detailed shopping lists. Remember: you can plan your changes and change your plans, so be flexible.

Shop smart

Try to shop wisely. If you do decide to cook using packet sauces, pastes or recipe mixes for convenience, make sure you read the labels and choose those lower in salt, sugar and fat. Favour the healthier options for convenience foods. Refer to the 'Understanding Food Labels' chapter in the *AHSG* to help you decipher other words for salt, sugar and fat that may be on the ingredients list.

Cooking marathons

Cooking marathons (or cook-ups) also save time, energy and money. By making extra during a marathon you can refrigerate or freeze meals for another day. You may even want to cook several dishes to last a few weeks at a time. If you can, invest in a large freezer to stock your supplies.

Dishes such as soups, spaghetti sauces, casseroles, stews and curries can be prepared ahead of time, popped in the freezer and then defrosted and reheated when required. This is a far better option than having takeaways, inappropriately snacking on high-kilojoule foods or having the same boring meal that you have already prepared several times that month.

Soups and casseroles may take a bit longer to prepare but you don't have to be standing over the stove stirring the whole time.

Waste not

Think about how you use your ingredients. Some recipes involve the same ingredient, for example evaporated skim milk for a cheesecake, stroganoff or creamy pasta sauce or canned tomatoes for a casserole or soup.

If you cook them at the same time you can use a whole packet or tin and save on waste.

Weekend blitz

Choose a Saturday or Sunday once a month (or half a day a fornight) to plan, shop and then cook up a storm. With a small amount of planning and preparation you'll have a few options in the fridge or freezer to choose from. All you have to do is reheat and enjoy.

Add some life

Practice makes perfect in the kitchen, so don't be afraid to experiment with new ingredients and recipes. Making meals colourful and enticing means there'll be less temptation from chips and chocolate. Try these ideas:

- **CUT UNUSUAL SHAPES** Julienne strips of zucchini or carrots before steaming.

- **CONTRAST TEXTURES** Revitalise tired tastebuds by combining crunchy with creamy, for example fresh strawberries, vanilla yoghurt and flaked almonds.

- **VARY TEMPERATURE** Combine hot with cold, such as warm chicken salad.

- **CONTRAST FLAVOURS** Try spicy with bland, for example piquant curry with refreshing tzatziki (yoghurt and cucumber dip).

- **TASTE NEW FOODS** Be adventurous. Serve starfruit, Chinese cabbage, soybean curd (tofu), or smoked spiced mussels for an epicurean adventure.

take stock

Take stock of your pantry, fridge and freezer when your time and your budget allows. Toss out all products past their 'use by' date and give away or store out of sight any items that don't support your new goals. You need to make room for those that do.

ORDER your pantry so that you can see at a glance what you've got. By doing this, you won't end up with half a dozen packets or cans of one product and none of another. You can then easily decide which products you need to buy.

A well-organised pantry, fridge and freezer will help you to prepare meals quickly and efficiently because you have everything at hand. Basic pantry items can be transformed into satisfying and healthy meals at any time, particularly if they are boosted with fresh produce from the fridge.

Remember: you don't have to stop eating high-fat, high-sugar foods, you just need to restrict their intake.

Of course, you may need to take family members into consideration here. You can add products that others frequently use to the list below. Some examples might include diet jelly, low-joule cordial and quick and easy standby meals that you can prepare in a flash, such as baked beans or tomato-based pasta sauce.

Freezer essentials

- frozen peas, beans, corn, broadbeans, spinach and other vegetables
- single-serve sachets of frozen vegetables if you live alone
- frozen convenience healthy dinners (optional)
- extra serves of frozen soups, casseroles, pasta sauces and/or curries you've cooked in advance
- frozen berries or other fruits
- low-fat ice cream
- wholemeal or wholegrain bread
- chicken and/or turkey breasts

A well-organised pantry, fridge and freezer will help you to prepare meals quickly.

Pantry essentials

- dried herbs
- spices
- low-joule salad dressings
- low-fat sauces
- cold-pressed olive oil
- canola or olive oil spray
- sweeteners
- peppercorns
- sea salt
- curry powder
- basil pesto
- tomato paste
- stock
- vinegars
- salsa dressings
- mustards

- Worcestershire/ soy sauce
- minced garlic/ginger/ chilli
- fresh garlic
- curry paste
- unsweetened canned fruit
- canned corn
- canned legumes/ beans
- canned tomatoes
- canned tuna
- canned soups
- UHT long-life skim milk
- evaporated skim milk
- vegetable juice
- dried fruits

- 'no added sugar' jam/fruit spreads
- nut spreads
- gelatine
- wholemeal pasta
- brown or basmati rice
- wholegrain cereals
- oats
- wholemeal crispbreads
- cornflour
- baking powder
- wholemeal flour
- breadcrumbs
- tea
- unsalted nuts
- plain popcorn

Fridge essentials (check weekly)

- butter or margarine
- eggs
- low-fat milk
- 'no added sugar' jam/fruit spread

- light cream cheese
- 'no added sugar' low-fat yoghurt
- fresh fruit and vegetables

- fresh meat, chicken, fish
- fresh herbs
- reduced-fat or low-fat cheese

equip yourself

It's time to equip yourself for success in the kitchen. You'll find it easier to move toward your new health plans if you're armed with a positive attitude and the correct utensils.

If you fail to plan, you plan to fail. Set your plans in sand, not concrete, just in case you change your mind.

KITCHEN success requires the right equipment for the job. This doesn't mean you need the most expensive tools of the trade but you should buy utensils and equipment that make cooking tasks quicker and easier.

The list opposite includes all the utensils you'll need to cook the recipes in Part 2, *Healthy Cook*. If you have them on hand you'll get your meals prepared faster and with less fuss.

It's important to measure and weigh things carefully, especially if you are trying to reduce your weight or if you have a particular health condition. Quantities are important for kilojoule calculation, so use your measuring cups, spoons and kitchen scales rather than making a guess.

Keep equipment in good condition. Sharp knives can save you time, particularly if you're dicing vegetables for soup. They also let you slice more thinly, decreasing the portion size of certain foods, such as cheese and meat.

USE IT OR LOSE IT

■ Are your kitchen cupboards and drawers brimming with utensils and equipment you never use? Do you keep broken springform cake tins and rusty cheese graters just in case? Have a thorough spring clean and reorganise your useful kitchen items into logical order. Throw out anything you haven't used in the past six months. Good organisation increases your cooking efficiency, which in turn cuts down your time standing over the stove.

Tools of the trade

Cooking is simpler and faster when one has the right equipment on hand.
Following is a list of utensils and equipment that you'll use regularly in the kitchen.

- small non-stick frypan
- large deep non-stick frypan
- wok
- steamer
- set of three saucepans varying in size including one large enough for soups
- set of sharp knives
- set of measuring cups
- set of measuring spoons
- bowls of differing sizes
- colander
- strainer

- measuring jugs
- set of kitchen scales
- tongs
- slotted spoon
- large spoon
- whisk
- can opener
- timer
- chopping boards – wood and plastic
- vegetable peeler
- grater
- pastry brush
- roasting dish
- roasting rack to fit into a roasting dish
- non-stick baking trays

- muffin tins
- springform pan
- ovenproof dishes
- loaf tin
- wooden spoons
- oven bags, aluminium foil and absorbent paper
- egg poacher
- pressure cooker
- food processor or hand-held beater for blending soups
- hand-held beaters
- airtight containers
- pen to mark dates on frozen meals
- rice cooker

healthy eating

A healthy eating plan should always include a wide variety of foods that are low in fat (particularly saturated fat), low in sugar and salt, and high in fibre, vitamins and minerals.

Our bodies consist of 50% to 60% water.

Water is vital for good health. It provides all the fluid we need without the kilojoules found in other beverages. Aim for 8 glasses (2 litres) per day.

THE *Australian Healthy Cooking Guide* encourages you to prepare, cook and eat healthy foods following the *Dietary guidelines for Australians* produced by the Australian government (see opposite).

It is recommended that you eat mostly unprocessed food from the major food groups, including wholegrains, fruit and vegetables, dairy, meat and meat substitutes and oils, and that you limit fat, salt, sugar and alcohol intake.

As part of the *chOOz to lOOz* progam, and in accordance with the dietary guidelines, I encourage you to eat 'free' or unrestricted vegetables (see list on page 174) to add bulk, nutrition and variety to recipes.

The vegetables that appear on the list have minimal kilojoules yet they contribute to the total energy or kilojoule count. You can eat as much of them as you like, within reason. Remember: balance is the key.

THIRSTY?

■ Water – enjoy it with a squeeze of lemon or lime.

■ Coffee and tea are stimulants, so enjoy them in moderation.

■ Restrict soft drinks and cordials as they are high in sugar and 'empty' kilojoules. Have 'diet' soft drinks and cordials sometimes to add variety, if desired.

Dietary guidelines for Australians

Enjoy a wide variety of nutritious foods:
○ Eat plenty of vegetables, legumes and fruits
○ Eat plenty of cereals, including breads, rice, pasta and noodles, preferably wholegrain
○ Include lean meat, fish, poultry and/or alternatives
○ Include milk, yoghurt, cheeses and/or alternatives. Reduced-fat varieties should be chosen where possible
○ Drink plenty of water

Take care to:
○ Limit saturated fat and moderate total fat intake
○ Choose foods low in salt
○ Limit your alcohol intake if you choose to drink
○ Consume moderate amounts of sugars and foods containing sugars

Prevent weight gain:
○ Be physically active and eat according to your energy needs

Care for your food:
○ Prepare and store it safely
○ Encourage and support breastfeeding

©Dietary guidelines for Australians, National Health and Medical Research Council, 2003. Commonwealth of Australia

take care

The old adage states 'everything in moderation', but when it comes to salt, fat and sugar it is better to live by 'the less you use, the better'.

Did you know?

Homemade stock is the lowest salt alternative when cooking soups, casseroles and sauces.

Salt-reduced liquid stock and stock powder have half the salt content of the standard variety.

Reconstituted stock cubes have similar salt content to commercial liquid stock.

Cut back salt

Salt (sodium chloride) is present naturally in many foods and is added to others to enhance flavour.

All recipes in the *AHCG* are suitable if you have high blood pressure or want to reduce salt intake. However, recipes marked with a salt symbol are best adapted by following the tips below for some of the ingredients in the book.

It is always best to use homemade stock in soups and casseroles, but feel free to use commercial stock alternatives for speed and convenience. Make sure you choose the best low-salt options by checking the *AHSG* for suggestions of the best brands.

Experiment with different seasonings such as lime or lemon juice, flavoured vinegars, pepper or herbs to liven up your meals without resorting to the salt shaker.

Clever ways to reduce salt

- **REPLACE SALT** Use onion or garlic powder in your salt shaker instead.

- **BUY REDUCED-SALT PRODUCTS** Look for reduced-salt baked beans, canned tuna and salmon, tomato soup, soy sauce, bread and margarine. They contain half the salt content of standard commercial brands.

- **USE REDUCED-SALT TOMATO PASTE** Also look for no-salt canned tomatoes. These contain less than 10% of the salt of standard varieties.

- **DRAIN THE BRINE** Pour off salty brine from canned food such as legumes, beans, salmon and tuna. Rinse the contents with water to remove excess salt.

- **LIMIT SALTY FOODS** Take care with processed foods such as bacon and foods naturally high in salt like prawns.

Not so sweet

Sugar in any form can add a lot of extra kilojoules. Sugar is 'empty' energy in that it doesn't add any beneficial nutrients to the diet. It can also over-stimulate the tastebuds, making it hard to stop once you start.

If you suffer from diabetes or are watching your weight, it is essential to restrict sugar to a minimum.

If you can't give up soft drinks or cordials, try 'diet' varieties. Cut down on biscuits, cakes and pastries – not only are they high in sugar, but most are also high in fat (unless you make your own healthy varieties).

Flour versus fat

Flour is not the villain when cooking stews or casseroles. Removing or reducing the fat is far more important than worrying about a thickening agent such as flour or cornflour. Where possible, use wholemeal flour rather than white – it's higher in fibre and nutrients.

DON'T WHINE ABOUT WINE

■ When you cook with wine, the alcohol evaporates yet the flavour is retained. The good news? The kilojoules evaporate too!

Clever ways to reduce sugar

- **BEWARE OF 'FAT FREE' SNACKS** Products that claim this status are often loaded with sugar and high in kilojoules if you read the fine print.

- **USE ARTIFICIAL SWEETENERS** Some recipes, including some dessert and cake recipes in *AHCG*, use artificial sweeteners rather than sugar.

- **TAKE CARE WITH HONEY, RAW OR BROWN SUGAR OR MOLASSES** Be aware that these 'natural' sugars contain essentially the same nutritional and energy content as sugar.

Remember: the message is not to cut out sugar, salt and fat entirely, just limit them.

limit the fat

The Australian dietary guidelines encourage us to limit saturated fats and moderate our total fat intake. All fats are high in kilojoules, so you need to trim it from your diet if you want to slim down.

EVERYONE needs some fat in their diet. Eating small amounts of the healthier fats, found in mono- or polyunsaturated vegetable oils and margarines, and in avocadoes, nuts and seeds, ensures we receive essential fatty acids and vitamins for good health.

Saturated fats are not essential to our wellbeing. They are found in full-fat dairy products, fatty meats and many fried takeaways.

Clever ways to reduce fat

1 Remove all the visible fat from meat, and the skin and fat from chicken, before cooking.

2 Cook meat or chicken so that the fat drains away as you cook and try not to add extra fat during the cooking process. Grilling, rack-roasting or steaming are good methods. Dry-fry using a non-stick pan or use a spray oil when browning meat for a casserole.

3 If light frying, measure fat carefully and aim to give no more than one teaspoon of margarine, butter or oil per person or one tablespoon for a family of four.

4 Use flavoured vinegar, lemon juice or lime juice as a salad dressing instead of oil or mayonnaise. For convenience, use commercial salad dressings that are low-oil or no-oil. Check the *AHSG* for suggestions on the best brands.

5 Use natural yoghurt or ricotta cheese flavoured with chopped chives instead of butter or sour cream on potato. Try flavoured cottage cheese, low-fat mayonnaise or flavoured light cream cheese.

All recipes in Part 2, *Healthy Cook* are suitable for those with elevated blood cholesterol levels. However, some recipes are marked with a symbol denoting that they may be adapted to further reduce the saturated fat content (see point 8 below).

FAT FILE

■ A diet low in saturated and trans fats is best for health.

■ Use monounsaturated and polyunsaturated oils and margarines, such as olive, canola, safflower and sunflower, and limit butter, especially if your blood cholesterol is high.

6 Low-fat cheeses such as ricotta can be substituted for cream in most dessert recipes.

7 Avoid baked vegetables unless they are dry-baked on a rack. You can do this by spraying lightly with a spray oil or by cooking in aluminium foil.

8 Choose low-fat dairy products where possible such as low-fat milk, yoghurt, cheese and ice cream. This is particularly important if you are watching your blood cholesterol level. For further details to help you select the type(s) that are best for you, refer to pages 34 to 37.

9 Smear butter or margarine thinly on bread or crispbreads – or leave it off altogether. Find alternatives to give flavour and moisture. Butter substitutes include plain or flavoured cottage cheese or light cream cheese. Add low-kilojoule condiments such as a thin scrape of *Vegemite*, fish or vegetable spread, mustard, salsa, horseradish, pickle or relish.

10 Use a little less fat than recipes recommend when making sauces, casseroles or in baking. Thirty grams less fat can save you a whopping 1081 kilojoules!

vegetables & fruit

It is recommended that you get at least five serves of vegies and two serves of fruit a day. Ideally, your dinner plate should be half vegetables or salad, a quarter protein foods like meat, chicken or fish and a quarter starchy carbs like potato, rice or pasta.

One serve of vegies = ½ cup of cooked veg or 1 cup of salad.

In disguise

Sneak vegetables into pasta sauces, patties, casseroles and soups by dicing or grating them, so that fussy eaters can't identify them.

MOST vegetables and salads contain many important vitamins (especially A and C), minerals, fibre and antioxidants. You can enjoy them without worrying about putting on weight. They are low in kilojoules and fat, unless you drown salads in mayonnaise, cook vegetables in oil, or pour creamy sauces over them, thus tripling the kilojoules!

Non-starchy green and orange vegetables are tops for health. They add nutrition and bulk to meals and help with weight control because their fibre acts as a natural appetite brake.

Frozen vegetables can be just as nutritious as fresh. They are picked at their prime, snap frozen very soon after harvesting and retain their nutrients.

The best ways to cook vegetables for nutrition and flavour are microwaving, steaming and stir-frying. If you boil vegetables, you pour the water-soluble vitamins down the drain with the water. Leave the skin on where possible – many nutrients are just under it and the skin itself is rich in fibre. Here's a tip: hold the salt and give vegetables a lift by adding a clove of garlic,

FRUIT FOR THOUGHT

■ Versatile fruit is more than just a snack. Enjoy it as a topping with your breakfast cereal, in a salad, as a dessert or in smoothies. It is more satisfying and filling to eat an apple with the fibre than to drink the juice. If you are watching your weight or blood glucose levels, be careful with dried fruit and juice, as it is easy to overdo it. One serve of fruit equals 30g dried fruit or half a cup (125ml) of unsweetened juice/canned fruit.

finely diced onion, fresh herbs, nutmeg, black pepper or onion powder.

The best things in life are free and that includes many vegetables. On page 174 you'll find my 'free' or unrestricted list of vegetables. If you are watching your weight or have diabetes, keep these in the fridge to snack on (with fat-free salsa or other free condiments) to help you deal with between-meal hunger pains. Or use them to fill up (and out) your midday and evening meals as salads or cooked vegetables – they add bulk without many kilojoules. Be creative too. Add them to stews, curries, soups, pasta sauces and salads even if they aren't on the ingredient list – they extend the meal and help you save on meat bills. And when it's party time, free vegetables make a perfect platter with a low-fat dip.

Be a savvy shopper

- **USE YOUR SENSES** Smell, look, feel and bend before you buy. Fruit and vegetables should be bright, colourful and intense in colour. Generally, they should be firm and should not bend easily, particularly vegetables such as carrots, zucchinis and cucumbers. If you aren't sure, buy one and taste. I sometimes buy an apple, taste it and if it is really good, I buy a few kilos.

- **GO FOR THE BACK ROW** Take your pick from the vegetable and fruit trays at the back – this is often where the freshest ones are.

- **SEASONS GREETINGS** Choose fresh fruit and vegetables in season when they are at their best and usually cheaper.

- **MAKE FRIENDS** Get to know the staff as they can tell you when fresh deliveries come in and what's best for eating right now.

- **GO ONLINE** If you can't get what you want locally, then let your fingers do the walking. Order over the phone, or online! I find this an invaluable money and time saver.

Dry-fry, steam or microwave vegetables so they are just crisp. This way they retain their colour, flavour and nutrients.

pasta

Grain foods like pasta, noodles, rice, bread and breakfast cereals are high in complex carbs and fibre (especially the wholegrain and wholemeal ones) and mostly low in fat.

Carbs are your body's most efficient fuel source.

Cook tomorrow's pasta sauce today. Reheating intensifies the flavours and it tastes even better.

THERE are wonderful varieties of fresh and dried pasta available. Wholemeal and vegetable-based pastas are best because they are higher in fibre and nutrients. Serve them as a main course or as an accompaniment

Be cautious with sauces. Tomato-based sauces tend to be lower in fat and kilojoules than creamy sauces. It's also best to make the sauce yourself. Homemade sauces are more filling, nutritious and lower in salt and sugar.

If you have to use commercial brands, look for 97% fat-free brands. Check the *AHSG* for suggestions. Here's a tip to make simple tomato-based sauces special.

Add vegetables, extra nutrients and filling power with zucchini, grated carrot, mushroom, eggplant and spinach or anything from the 'free' vegetables list (page 174). Herb it up with basil, oregano or marjoram. Make extra pasta sauce and freeze in portions for a rainy day.

BAKE IT

■ Pasta bakes with lots of vegetables make a great meal in a dish. Place alternating layers of lasagne sheets and a vegetable-based sauce (add spinach or silverbeet) in a baking dish. Top with a low-fat white sauce flavoured with a small amount of tasty or parmesan cheese. Bake in a moderate oven for 30 minutes.

rice

Rice is a versatile grain. It's the perfect accompaniment to stir-fries and curries and makes a complete meal mixed with protein, vegetables and herbs to create creamy risottos or mornays.

HOWEVER you enjoy it, rice is low in fat and a good source of complex carbs and fibre, especially if you choose brown rice with its healthy wholegrain nutrition. Don't be put off thinking that brown rice takes forever to cook. Some of the new quick-cooking varieties are ready in half the time required for regular brown rice.

If you are watching your weight or blood glucose levels, you may want to choose lower GI rices like basmati, Doongara Clever Rice and Moolgiri, or try a wild rice blend.

Give rice a flavour boost by cooking it in a low-fat stock instead of water.

Rice plus vegies makes ...

- **EASY FRIED RICE** Add mixed frozen or fresh vegetables to cooked rice.

- **HEALTHY RISOTTO** Add asparagus, peas or other vegetables to risottos and serve as a side dish. Use lean chicken, mushrooms and spring onions and serve with salad as a main meal.

- **FRAGRANT PILAF** Add mixed frozen or fresh vegetables, spices and flaked almonds to the rice while cooking.

BROWN-SHIFTING

If you'd prefer to make a gradual transition to brown rice, try combining it with white. Add brown rice to boiling water, cook for 15 minutes, then add white rice and cook for a further 15 minutes.

potatoes

Potatoes and sweet potatoes are starchy vegetables which is why they aren't on the 'free' list. Enjoy them as an accompaniment – an average serve is one medium potato.

> Bring back potatoes! Eat them mashed, steamed or baked but not deep-fried as chips or swimming in butter.

POTATOES come in different sizes, shapes and colours, so don't stick with the same ones all the time. Many varieties of potato have a high GI, so if you are diabetic or watching your blood glucose levels or weight you may prefer orange sweet potatoes as they have a moderate GI. Steaming, microwaving or baking are the best ways to cook potatoes to retain the nutrients. But avoid high-fat roast potatoes. Here are my suggestions for baking potatoes (and other vegetables too) with a minimum of fat (or none at all):

- Wrap in foil and bake in a moderate oven until soft – about 1 hour.
- Steam or boil until tender, spray them with a cooking spray and bake in a hot oven until crispy.

POTATO TOPPERS

These potato-topping alternatives to butter or sour cream won't blow your kilojoule budget. Try:

■ Plain or flavoured cottage cheese sprinkled with garlic chives or parsley.

■ Low-fat or extra-light cream cheese mixed with grainy or Dijon mustard.

■ Low-fat or no-fat plain yoghurt on its own or mixed with herbs, mustard powder or spices like ginger, cinnamon and cloves.

■ Light sour cream mixed with chopped spring onions.

breakfast cereals

Breakfast cereals aren't just for breakfast. You can enjoy a bowl of cereal as a snack, as a dessert or for supper. There are no rules.

WHERE possible, choose high-fibre, wholegrain cereals that are lower in fat and 'added sugars'. This is why it's important to read the ingredient list on the back of the packet. You also need to check the nutrition information panel. Generally, look for cereals that provide less than 25g of total sugar per 100g if there is fruit in the ingredients. As there are well over 200 breakfast cereals on the market, you may want to use my *AHSG* to help you choose a healthy high-fibre option that suits the whole family. Remember, starting the day with a high-fibre cereal sets you well on the road to achieving the 30g of fibre you need every day to help keep you regular.

Watch portion sizes. Heavier cereals (by weight) such as muesli may be heavier in kilojoules too. Don't fill up your bowl with them, especially if you are watching your weight. Top with sliced fresh fruit instead.

Go for wholegrain and get the fibre and nutrients.

Mix and match

- **MIX IT** Add variety and flavour to breakfast by mixing two cereals together. For a fibre boost, include a very high-fibre cereal, like half a cup of *All-Bran* or two *Hi-Bran Weet-Bix* to get at least an extra 8g of fibre a day.

- **MATCH IT** Add healthy toppings to your cereal to boost the nutritional value and flavour. Try dried, stewed or sliced fresh fruit or unsweetened canned fruit. Use low-fat milk and yoghurt.

- **MAKE IT** Make a creamy porridge with rolled oats using half low-fat milk and half water. Add sultanas or mashed banana and top with cinnamon.

bread & crackers

Breads, crumpets, muffins, crackers and crispbreads are low-fat carbs that form the basis of many easy meals and quick snacks. Choose wholegrain or unrefined varieties – they have a higher fibre and roughage content to keep your digestive system healthy.

Most adults need at least 30g of fibre per day for optimal bowel health.

Did you know?
Bread is not a forbidden food. It's more a case of what is put on the bread that leads to an excessive energy intake rather than the bread itself.

WHOLEGRAIN breads and crackers take longer to eat and are more satisfying than their refined white cousins. Look for nutrient-rich dark rye, pumpernickel, mixed grains, kibble wheat and wholemeal varieties.

Dry biscuits, crackers, muffins, crumpets and pita or Mountain bread can be substituted for run-of-the-mill bread, especially if you're trying to liven up lunchtime. Topped with low-fat dip or meat, cheese, chicken, tuna and fresh salad ingredients, breads and crackers become quick, delicious and easy light meals and snacks.

Remember to check the supermarket for brands that are lower in fat, salt and sugar. Use the *AHSG* to help you choose wisely.

HIT THE RIGHT LEVEL

■ Are you watching your weight or blood sugar levels? Try to control snack and meal sizes carefully. Add a dairy option or a low-fat, protein-based food such as meat or egg to help you stay fuller for longer.

■ If you have high blood pressure or need to watch your salt intake look for crispbreads lower in salt.

Healthy bread and crackers

- **PIZZA MUFFINS** Top a wholemeal English muffin with lean ham, cheese, capsicum and mushrooms.

- **SPREAD IT ON** Spread toasted wholegrain bread with a nutritious topping such as low-salt peanut paste or light cream cheese

- **TOAST OF THE TOWN** Use a jaffle-maker or sandwich toaster to make a low-fat cheese and tomato snack with wholemeal bread.

- **TASTY CRUMPETS** Spread wholemeal crumpets or muffins with light cream cheese and 100% fruit spread. For a savoury treat, try a light scraping of *Vegemite* and a slice of low-fat cheese.

- **FLAT-OUT FEAST** Try a pikelet or pancake with 100% fruit spread. (See pancake recipe, page 151).

- **DIP INTO IT** Have wholemeal crackers, crispbreads, rice cakes or corn cakes spread with low-fat dips and condiments.

- **CRISP AND LIGHT** Make pita crisps. Cut the bread into wedges, pop them in the oven and bake for 5 minutes until crisp. Serve with a low-fat dip.

- **AFTERNOON DELIGHT** Toast raisin bread or fruit loaf as an afternoon snack. Choose 'no added sugar' varieties, particularly if you're watching your blood sugar level.

- **WISE SNACKS** Snack on low-fat *Snakatas* or unsalted pretzels. You can purchase some products in multi-packs for work or school lunchboxes.

- **WRAP IT UP** Fill pita pockets or Mountain bread with healthy ingredients such as grated carrot, shredded lettuce, reduced-fat cheese, hummus dip, tuna, salmon, lean chicken or roast beef.

- **SWEET TREAT** Serve warm scones with 100% fruit spread.

meat

Meat is high in protein, iron, zinc and other minerals and vitamins. However, it may contain considerable fat and kilojoules. Keep an eye on serving sizes, especially if you are trying to control your weight or fat intake.

Trim any visible fat from meat before cooking.

Check the ratings in the AHSG before buying processed meats to make sure you buy brands that are lower in salt and fat.

CHOOSE lean cuts of meat, and restrict fatty meats such as bacon, sausages, marbled meat and processed meat including salami. Most lean cuts of beef, pork and lamb are suitable. Look particularly for 'new fashion' pork and trim lamb as these are leaner cuts.

If using mince meat, prepare your own using lean meat or look for commercial lean weight-watchers or premium mince with little fat content or ask your butcher to mince some lean meat especially for you.

Freeze as soon as possible as there will be no preservatives to keep it fresh.

A serve of 90 to120g cooked meat is plenty for a main meal for most adults, so for a family of four you only need to buy about 500g raw meat. You can extend meaty casseroles, soups, stir fries or spaghetti sauces with plenty of free vegetables even if they aren't in the recipe – they balance meals and add bulk without extra kilojoules while the 'extra' size of the meal will please your eyes and satisfy your stomach.

On the rack
Roast meats on a rack in a baking tray filled with a little water. Rub the meat with herbs or condiments and then cover tightly with foil to keep the meat moist. Rosemary works well with lamb or try chopped sage leaves with pork. Don't forget to remove the foil about 20 minutes before the finish time to allow the meat to brown.

Cut the fat

How you prepare and cook meat really matters. Cooking even lean cuts of meat with fat or oil of any kind can easily double or triple the kilojoules. So measure carefully!

- Cook meat on a rack if baking or grilling so that the fat drips away.

- Trim all visible fat from meat before you cook it.

- To seal or brown meat for casseroles, dry-fry using a non-stick pan or non-stick cooking spray, or use minimal fat. You can achieve the same browning effect by 'froiling' or frying the meat in a small amount of water.

- Cook casseroles, stews, soups and stocks the day before and store them in the fridge overnight. Any fat will rise to the top and set so that you can remove it before reheating the food.

- If microwaving meat, cook it slowly on a plastic rack so more fat can drain away.

- Cook fatty cuts or mince, then allow the dish to cool before removing the fat. You can add a little thickening such as cornflour when reheating if desired.

- If you use oven bags, don't add any extra fat and don't use the juices for gravy, without removing the fat first.

POTATOES WITH YOUR ROAST?

■ Don't cook potatoes or other vegetables in the same dish that the meat is cooking in – they'll soak up any fat like a sponge. Instead, wrap them separately in aluminium foil and remove this in the last ten minutes, spray lightly with low-fat oil and sprinkle with paprika to brown.

If you wish to fry, use a non-stick fry pan or a non-stick cooking spray.

chicken

Chicken and turkey are high in protein, vitamins and minerals and low in fat and salt if you choose lean, fresh cuts. Skinned chicken or turkey breasts are the lowest in fat.

Remove all skin and fat from chicken before cooking, especially fat near the tail and neck.

A serve of 90 to 120g of cooked meat is right for most adults as a main meal.

MAKING a casserole or wrapping and baking in foil are good ways to cook skinless chicken to prevent it from drying out. It becomes very tender cooked slowly in casseroles with different herb and vegetable combinations.

To bake, season the skinless chicken pieces first, add a squeeze of lemon juice for a tangy flavour then wrap in foil. When grilling or barbecuing, season and marinate chicken pieces or kebabs before cooking for a more flavoursome dish. Basting with the marinade during cooking keeps the meat moister. Cut back salt and add more flavour with herbs and spices. For example, combine coriander, tarragon or curry powder with lemon juice and brush over chicken before cooking.

WRAPT

■ If you make or buy chicken parcels, opt for low-fat fillings such as breadcrumbs and herbs; pineapple and lean ham; mushroom and light cream cheese; spinach, ricotta cheese and light cream cheese; salsa or tomato, basil and parmesan cheese. Avoid parcels packed with butter, cheese or bacon as well as those wrapped in bacon. You can wrap chicken in filo pastry before baking parcels because filo is fat free. Spray the filo with a non-stick cooking spray to separate the layers and then spray the outside of the parcel to help it brown.

fish

Fish is low in saturated fat and the Omega-3 fats that it does contain have been shown to have numerous health benefits. That's why you should try to include fish or seafood in your diet at least twice a week.

WHEN selecting fresh fish, look for shining scales and eyes, firm flesh and no fishy odour. If you buy frozen fish or seafood, thaw it in the fridge and never re-freeze.

If you are unsure about healthy ways to prepare fish, catch my cooking tips. Remember, fish is cooked when the flesh flakes easily with a fork. Be sure not to let it dry out. Season whole fish or fillets first and moisten with lemon or lime juice or white wine during cooking.

Canned salmon or tuna are handy for salads, sandwiches and fish patties. Choose varieties canned in brine, spring water or tomato (or barbecue) sauce. If you are trying to reduce your salt intake, choose fish canned in spring water or look for 'no added salt' on the label.

> Season fish with lemon, lime, garlic, coriander, ginger, tarragon, lemongrass, onion powder, black pepper or soy sauce.

Catch these cooking tips

- **GRILL** Place whole fish or fillets on foil, sprinkle with lemon juice, season and cook under a griller.

- **BAKE** Season fish, add a little lemon, lime, tomato juice or white wine, then wrap in foil and bake.

- **POACH** Simmer in a pan fish or smoked fish just covered with water, milk or stock.

- **STEAM** Place fish on a plate on top of a saucepan of boiling water. Season and sprinkle with lemon juice, cover with a second plate and cook.

cheese

Dairy foods include cow's milk, cheese and yoghurt. Choose reduced-fat options where possible, particularly if you are watching your blood cholesterol level.

CHEESE (as well as milk and yoghurt) provides many nutrients including protein, calcium, magnesium and phosphorus. It's best to choose lower fat varieties from the fresh, firm and hard categories, as many soft cheeses are high in saturated fat.

Reducing fat

If you are on a cholesterol-lowering or low-fat diet, it is particularly important to choose cheeses with a lower fat content. The nutrition information panel on the wrapper or packet displays the grams of fat per 100 grams. Some brands are as low as 2 grams of fat per 100 grams. Ideally, aim for not more than 10 grams of fat per 100 grams (or 10% fat).

If you are watching your weight and you dislike the taste of reduced-fat or low-fat cheese, use regular tasty cheese sliced thinly.

Use a vegetable peeler to make slivers of tasty cheese go further or grate it for sandwiches or to use in cooking. Sharp-tasting cheeses such as tasty and parmesan mean you get loads of flavour without having to use as much.

Fresh cheese

Fresh cheeses are perishable and not matured. There are two types: low-fat cottage and ricotta cheese, and cream cheese. Low-fat cottage, low-fat ricotta and lower fat cream cheeses such as *Philadelphia* light or extra light cream cheese are the best choices.

If you are following a very low-fat or cholesterol-lowering diet, low-fat cottage, ricotta or extra light cream cheeses are the best, as they are all less than 5% fat. Choose fresh cheeses if you are following a low-salt diet.

> ### Did you know?
> Even though reduced-fat cheese is lower in fat than full-fat hard cheese, it still has around 25% fat.

Hard cheese

The reduced-fat and low-fat hard cheeses are lower in fat and kilojoules than the full-fat, matured hard cheeses. They can be used in larger serving amounts as a substitute for meat and are valuable to include in a weight-reducing or cholesterol-lowering program.

If you are watching your cholesterol level, aim for hard cheese with less than 10% fat.

The *AHSG* will assist you in understanding food labels and which cheese brands are best to use. Check for the brands that provide lower fat options if you are watching your weight or blood cholesterol levels.

Say cheese

- **SNACK WELL** Substitute cottage cheese for butter on sandwiches, toast and crispbreads. Spread *Vegemite*, *Promite*, fish or vegetable spread thinly on the bread first, then top with cottage cheese, tomato and salad.

- **FRUITY CHEESE** Serve ricotta or cottage cheese on fruit or in celery sticks.

- **TOP SPUDS** Baked potatoes taste great with ricotta or cottage cheese instead of butter or sour cream. Sprinkle chopped chives, Spanish onion or your favourite fresh herbs on top.

- **CHEESEY SALADS** Serve cheese with salad vegetables as a refreshing and simple summer meal.

- **GRILL IT** Enjoy grilled cheese on toast, vegetables or crackers. Melt cheese on dry crackers by placing them in a microwave for 30 seconds. It's great for a cold day and melting it makes your cheese go further!

- **SLICE IT** Make cheese go further by grating or 'peeling' it into thin slices with a vegetable peeler. This makes a little seem like a great deal more, especially in salads and on sandwiches.

- **SAUCY CHEESE** Make a silky cheese sauce by thickening low-fat or skim milk with cornflour instead of the *roux* method using flour and butter. Add a little parmesan or grated low-fat cheese, chives, parsley and pepper for extra flavour. Use cheese sparingly and preferably use the lower fat varieties. Curry powder, mustard powder or a chicken stock cube are alternatives that can cut down fat and kilojoules further if used in place of cheese.

milk

Most people should be aiming for three serves of dairy foods per day. Alternatives to fresh milk include non-fat powdered milk, low-fat evaporated canned milk and low-fat longlife milk.

SOY FAR, SOY GOOD

■ Soy milk has less calcium than cow's milk, so choose soy milk that is fortified with calcium. Preferably choose low-fat if you are watching your weight.

Fresh milk

Low-fat fresh milk has less than 2% fat, less than half the amount of fat found in full-cream milk and less than three-quarters of the kilojoules. There are several low-fat, low-sugar flavoured milks now available.

Non-fat or skim milk has less than 0.1% fat and around half the kilojoules of whole milk and is the best option if you are watching your cholesterol level.

Powdered non-fat milk

Powdered milk contains no fat, has half the kilojoules of regular milk yet retains the protein and calcium. It is also the least expensive form of milk and is easy to make up when required – no more sour milk!

Longlife skim milk is actually non-fat milk and has a similar composition to non-fat powdered milk. Keep it in your pantry to use at a moment's notice.

Milking it

- **SILKY SMOOTHIES** Blend low-fat milk with fruit and yoghurt. Try frozen or fresh mixed berries and a banana blended with vanilla yoghurt and a sprinkle of nutmeg.

- **DESSERT DELIGHTS** Use low-fat milk in custard, creamed rice, bread-and-butter pudding and junket.

- **SOUPS AND SAUCES** Add milk for a creamy soup or a cheese sauce. Try skim evaporated milk for a more concentrated creamy taste to replace cream.

yoghurt

Choose low-fat plain or low-fat flavoured yoghurt. If you prefer fruit-flavoured yoghurt, choose low-fat brands labelled 'no added sugar', particularly if you are watching your weight or your blood sugar levels.

Healthy yoghurt

- **BREAKFAST BONUS** Try low-fat plain or flavoured yoghurt on your breakfast cereal instead of or as well as milk.

- **SUBSTITUTE FOR CREAM** Try low-fat, low-sugar vanilla yoghurt as a topping for fresh or stewed fruit or other desserts. You can also flavour plain low-fat yoghurt with vanilla, cinnamon and a non-sugar sweetener.

- **YOGHURT DIP** Serve Greek tzatziki dip made with yoghurt, cucumber, mint and garlic. You can also try it as an accompaniment to curry.

- **YOGHURT CHICKEN** Use plain low-fat yoghurt in baked chicken dishes such as tandoori chicken for a delicious, mildly spicy Indian dish.

- **DOLLOP ON A POTATO** Add chopped fresh herbs, sprinkle with spice mix or chilli flakes.

- **CASSEROLE ADD-IN** Use yoghurt in stroganoffs in place of cream. Don't let it boil – add it toward the end of cooking while simmering slowly.

SUPER-DUPER YOGHURT

Eating it straight from the tub is a healthy snack, but try new ways to eat low-fat yoghurt. It's delicious in dips, desserts and cooking.

eggs

Eggs are nutritious, rich in protein and a delicious meat substitute. The many varieties include eggs high in Omega-3s.

ECONOMICAL and versatile, eggs are the basis for many interesting light meals, including omelettes and frittatas. Include them at breakfast, lunch or dinner in a variety of ways to ensure you beat the boredom factor.

Eggs can be an ideal meat substitute for vegetarians. If you are are watching your blood cholesterol or weight you can include protein-rich eggs as part of your diet, but be careful how you cook them. Frying in oil or butter increases the fat and kilojoule count. Scramble eggs with a dash of low-fat milk, or poach or boil them for a healthy breakfast or snack.

Healthy eggs

- **BOILED** Boil water in a small saucepan. Add eggs gently and simmer for 3 to 4 minutes.

- **POACHED** Add 1 teaspoon of lemon juice or vinegar to a pan of simmering water. Break the eggshells and open carefully as close as possible to the surface of the water; gently slide the eggs in. Simmer for 3 to 5 minutes. Lift the eggs out carefully with an egg slice to drain.

- **SCRAMBLED** Allow two eggs per person and 1 tablespoon of milk for each egg. Season with pepper and onion powder (a good substitute for salt) and beat lightly. Cook by stirring over a low heat in a non-stick pan or one with non-stick spray until the eggs are just set.

FLUFFIER OMELETTES

Omelettes are fluffier if you separate the yolks and whites and beat them separately. Season and add 1 tablespoon of milk for each egg yolk and fold the whites into the yolks. Heat a non-stick pan or lightly spray a pan with cooking oil and spread the egg mixture evenly into the pan. Cook over a low heat until it puffs. Place under a hot griller until the top is set, fold over, serve and enjoy.

beans & legumes

More and more people are choosing to eat a vegetarian meal once or twice a week. Legumes such as beans and lentils provide valuable vitamins and minerals and are a good source of iron and protein.

LEGUMES are also low in fat, high in fibre and won't break the kilojoule budget. Including more of them in your diet can help reduce high blood cholesterol.

Dried or canned, you can use beans, chickpeas, lentils and split peas in a whole range of dishes including soups, stews, stir-fries and salads. You can serve them as an accompaniment or use them to extend meat dishes. For a quick, sustaining meal it's hard to beat baked beans on high-fibre toast sprinkled with low-fat cheese.

Many special vegetarian foods are made from beans, especially soy beans – tofu, for example, is soy bean curd. Look for vegetarian products that are lower in fat and salt when shopping. Check the *AHSG* for information on the healthier options.

Can do with canned beans

- **DIP THEM** Blend chickpeas with lemon juice, garlic, tahini and a little water.

- **MASH THEM** Combine cannellini beans with cooked mashed potato and a little low-fat yoghurt.

- **PURÉE THEM** Blend white beans with hot chicken stock and herbs to serve with steamed vegetables.

- **TOSS THEM** Add three bean mix to salads for colour, flavour and texture.

- **BLEND THEM** Purée kidney beans with tomato paste for a pizza/pita spread.

If preparing dried beans, change the soaking water and rinse well before cooking to help beat the gas. And don't add salt – it can toughen them. Cooked beans freeze well. Keep some as a healthy standby.

2

Healthy Cook

adapt it

It can be a rewarding challenge to adapt favourite old recipes as well as interesting new ones to help reduce the kilojoules and create a healthier version.

YOUR main aim when trying to adapt recipes is to reduce the amount of fat, sugar and salt and, where possible, to increase the quantity of fibre, vitamins and minerals. Look for recipes with plenty of 'free' vegetables. You can always add more free vegies into your meals by including a salad or vegetable side dish, or by having an appetising 'free' soup to add bulk to a meal and help prevent overeating.

How to analyse recipes and choose ingredients

- **SWEET** Strive for minimal sugar, honey, fruit juice concentrate, molasses, corn syrup and golden syrup. Aim for less than one teaspoon or 5g of sweetener per serve. Experiment with artificial sweeteners.

- **FAT** Aim for minimal amounts of fat in the form of butter, margarine, oil, cream, fatty meat and chicken with skin, and limit serving sizes of nuts and full-fat cheese. Aim for no more than 1 teaspoon or 5g of added fat per serve, particularly if you are watching your weight.

- **FIBRE** Look specifically at those recipes with plenty of high-fibre foods such as vegetables, fruit, wholegrain rice, barley, oats, wholemeal flour, soybeans, kidney beans or other dried beans and peas.

- **SERVING SIZE** Control your serving sizes of meat and chicken, and starchy vegetables such potatoes, pasta and rice. To ensure you do not overeat, divide the ingredients in the recipe by the number of serves to determine how much of each ingredient is in one portion. For example, 500g of lean meat in a recipe for four people is equivalent to 125g of meat per person, which is a typical serve of meat.

Recipe symbols

The recipes in the *AHCG* contain no added sugar, are low in fat and kilojoules, and low to moderate in salt. All recipes are suitable for those wishing to lose or control their weight or for those with diabetes. All recipes are suitable, or can be adapted slightly to be suitable, for people with high blood pressure, for those trying to reduce their salt intake, for those with elevated blood cholesterol, and for those trying to further reduce their saturated fat intake. Use the suggestions throughout this book, and particularly those on pages 18, 19, 20, 21, 34, 35, 36 and 37 to achieve the nutritional benchmarks listed below.

C A recipe marked with this symbol can be adapted to be lower in saturated fat to achieve the nutritional benchmarks listed below.

S A recipe marked with this symbol can be adapted to be lower in sodium (salt) to achieve the nutritional benchmarks listed below.

Nutritional benchmarks

Saturated (sat) fat

- Appetisers, Desserts, Vegetables and Salads, Children's recipes: no more than 3g sat fat per serve

- Soups, Muffins and Cakes: no more than 1g sat fat per serve

- Main courses (including Meat, Chicken, Fish and Seafood, Vegetarian): no more than 5g sat fat per serve

Salt (sodium)

- Appetisers, Soups, Vegetables and Salads, Muffins and Cakes, Desserts, Children's recipes: no more than 300mg sodium per serve

- Main courses (including Meat, Chicken, Fish and Seafood, Vegetarian): no more than 600mg sodium per serve

Substitute standard bacon rashers in recipes with lean bacon, lean ham or smoked lean meats such as pastrami or smoked turkey breast.

All these recipes contain less than
890 KJ (215 calories) per serve.

Appetisers often have a high fat content – think crumbed prawns, pastries, quiches or pâtés. Here are tasty, low-fat and delicious recipes for entertaining or to eat as a healthy snack or a light lunch.

appetisers

appetisers

Tzatziki Dip with Pita Crisps
Serves 2

1 cup full-cream natural yoghurt

½ cup grated cucumber, moisture
  squeezed out

2 cloves garlic, crushed

1 tablespoon white vinegar

1 wholemeal Lebanese bread

olive oil or canola cooking spray

¼ teaspoon lemon pepper

paprika to taste

1 Place the yoghurt in a clean tea
  towel and allow it to hang on the
  tap in a sink, overnight.

2 Put the cucumber, yoghurt, garlic
  and vinegar into a bowl and
  mix well to combine. Cover and
  refrigerate until needed. Serve with
  pita chips.

3 Preheat the oven to 180°C. To make
  the pita crisps, cut the pita bread
  into wedges (approximately 8 large
  wedges). Place the wedges onto a
  baking tray, spray with the cooking
  spray and sprinkle with the lemon
  pepper and paprika.

4 Bake in the oven for 12–20 minutes
  or until crisp. Cool on a wire rack.
  Store in an airtight container. The
  crisps should last a week.

---

chOOz to lOOz Program
1 serve = 1 milk exchange 1 bread
exchange and ½ fat exchange

PER SERVE INCLUDING PITA CRISPS

KJ (cal)	813 (194)	Protein	10.1g
Fat	5.4g	Sodium	318mg
Saturated Fat	3.0g	Fibre	2.2g
Carbohydrate	23.2g		

Curried Ricotta Dip

Serves 4

200g reduced-fat ricotta cheese

½ cup celery, finely chopped

¼ cup sultanas

1 teaspoon curry powder

2 teaspoons lemon juice

3 medium apples, cut into thin wedges and dipped into lemon juice

1 Put the ricotta, celery, sultanas, curry powder and lemon juice into a bowl and mix well to combine.

2 Place in to a serving dish and refrigerate until ready to serve. Serve with the apple wedges.

> **chOOz to lOOz Program**
> 1 serve = 1 fruit exchange
> plus 1 milk exchange

PER SERVE INCL. VEGETABLE STICKS			
KJ (cal)	702 (168)	Protein	6.0g
Fat	4.6g	Sodium	112mg
Saturated Fat	2.8g	Fibre	3.4g
Carbohydrate	24.9g		

Corn Relish Dip

Serves 4

200g reduced-fat ricotta cheese

1 small jar or about 250g of corn relish

2 teaspoons parsley, finely chopped

1 wholemeal Lebanese bread, cut into 8 wedges

olive oil or canola spray

¼ teaspoon lemon pepper paprika

1 Preheat the oven to 180°C. Put the ricotta, corn relish and parsley into a bowl and mix well to combine.

2 Place into a serving dish and refrigerate until ready to serve.

3 Place the pita bread wedges onto a baking tray, spray with the cooking spray and sprinkle with the lemon pepper and paprika. Bake in the oven for 12–20 minutes or until crisp.

4 Cool on a wire rack. Store in an airtight container. The chips should last a week.

> **chOOz to lOOz Program**
> 1 serve = 1 meat exchange and
> 1 starchy vegetable exchange

PER SERVE INCLUDING PITA CHIPS			
KJ (cal)	792 (189)	Protein	8.4g
Fat	5.2g	Sodium	303mg
Saturated Fat	2.9g	Fibre	2.0g
Carbohydrate	26.3g		

appetisers

Salmon Dip with Vegetable Sticks
Serves 4

200g low-fat ricotta cheese

60g or 2 tablespoons canned salmon in brine, drained

4 chives, finely chopped

1 teaspoon lemon juice

4 sticks celery, cut into sticks

4 medium carrots, cut into sticks

1 Put the ricotta cheese, salmon, chives and lemon juice into a bowl and mix well to combine.

2 Transfer to a serving dish, cover and refrigerate until ready to serve.

3 Serve the dip with the vegetable sticks.

Garlic Bread
Serves 4

200g low-fat ricotta cheese

2 cloves garlic, crushed

8 slices wholemeal bread

1 Preheat oven to 200°C. Put the ricotta cheese and crushed garlic into a bowl and mix well to combine.

2 Spread the slices of bread with the ricotta garlic mixture and press the slices together.

3 Wrap the bread in foil and bake for 20 minutes until crisp and golden.

---

chOOz to lOOz Program
1 serve = 1 meat exchange

PER SERVE INCLUDING VEGETABLE			
KJ (cal)	465 (111)	Protein	9.2g
Fat	5.4g	Sodium	244mg
Saturated Fat	3.1g	Fibre	2.5g
Carbohydrate	5.2g		

S

chOOz to lOOz Program
1 serve = 2 bread exchanges
plus 1 meat exchange

PER SERVE			
KJ (cal)	890 (213)	Protein	11.4g
Fat	6.2g	Sodium	404mg
Saturated Fat	3.1g	Fibre	4.3g
Carbohydrate	25.5g		

Mushroom Pâté with Melba Toast

Serves 4

1 teaspoon olive oil

2 medium onions, finely chopped

500g mushrooms, finely chopped

3 teaspoons mild curry powder

1 tablespoon mixed herbs

¼ cup unprocessed bran

¼ cup wheat germ

6 drops Tabasco sauce

2 slices white bread

1. Preheat oven to 200°C. Lightly grease a small terrine dish.

2. Heat the oil in a non-stick fry pan, add the onions and mushrooms and cook over a medium heat for 20 minutes.

3. Put the curry powder, herbs, bran and wheat germ into a bowl. Add to the mushroom mixture with the Tabasco and mix well to combine.

4. Spoon the mixture into the prepared dish. Cover and bake for 1 hour. Allow to cool and refrigerate overnight. Invert the terrine onto a serving plate.

5. Toast the bread in triangles and serve with pâté.

> **chOOz to lOOz Program**
> 1 serve = 1½ bread exchanges

PER SERVE			
KJ (cal)	623 (149)	Protein	8.5g
Fat	2.9g	Sodium	101mg
Saturated Fat	0.5g	Fibre	7.2g
Carbohydrate	18.0g		

appetisers

Roasted Spicy Chickpeas
Serves 3

⅓ cup raw chickpeas

olive oil cooking spray

¼ teaspoon salt

¼ teaspoon chilli powder

1 Soak the chickpeas in water overnight. Drain well.

2 Preheat oven to 150°C. Place the chickpeas in a single layer on a baking tray lined with baking paper. Spray lightly with oil and sprinkle with the salt and chilli powder. Bake for around 45 to 60 minutes or until the chickpeas are crisp and golden. Shake the tray every 20 minutes to prevent the chickpeas sticking together.

3 Once cooked remove from the oven and allow to cool. Store chickpeas in an airtight container.

chOOz to lOOz Program
1 serve = 1 meat exchange

PER SERVE			
KJ (cal)	279 (67)	Protein	3.8g
Fat	1.3g	Sodium	208mg
Saturated Fat	0.2g	Fibre	2.8g
Carbohydrate	7.8g		

More quick and light bites ...

- **ASPARAGUS SPEARS** Steam and sprinkle lightly with low-oil French dressing or lemon juice and garnish with red capsicum.

- **CELERY BOATS** Chop celery into 5cm pieces and fill with one of the low-fat dip recipes from this chapter or with flavoured cottage cheese.

- **SMOKED SALMON ON PUMPERNICKEL** Top small rounds of pumpernickel bread with light cream cheese, thick slices of smoked salmon and sliced Spanish onion rings or capers.

- **MARINATED MUSHROOMS** Wipe small fresh mushrooms with a damp cloth and toss in lemon juice. Thirty minutes before serving, add a little low-oil French dressing, drain and serve.

- **CHEESE BALLS** Roll teaspoons of cottage or ricotta cheese into small balls and roll lightly in sesame seeds, poppy seeds, parsley or paprika. Serve well chilled, with toothpicks.

- **VEGETABLE DIPPERS** Use cut up vegetables such as capsicum strips, celery sticks, cucumber or carrot as an alternative to crackers. Serve with one of the commercial low-fat dip mixes from the *AHSG* or one of the dips from this chapter.

- **SKINNY DIP** Take a crushed stock cube, a packet of low-joule French onion soup or canned salmon then add one or more of the following: gherkins, herbs, garlic, onions or chives. Use as a dip with raw vegetables or crispbreads. You can also spread it on toast, sandwiches or crackers.

All these recipes contain less than 970KJ (232 calories) per serve. Many are actually less than 340KJ (80 calories) per serve and are classified as 'free' soups.

Nutritious and warming,
these delicious homemade
soups are perfect starters
or hearty one-pot meals.

soups

basic stocks

There is nothing quite like the flavour of a soup made on homemade stock. Allow a couple of hours on the weekend to make a big pot, divide it into portions and use as you need it. It'll be lucky to make it to the end of the week, especially in winter.

Free stock

All stocks referred to are free, as the fat is always skimmed after cooling.

Remember that if you include split peas, rice, barley, soup mix or noodles when you make soup from the stock, count these as a bread or starchy vegetable exchange.

If you include meat, chicken or legumes such as lentils or kidney beans, count these as a meat or protein exchange.

Most of the following soup recipes use liquid stock, stock cubes or powder for convenience.

Basic Meat or Chicken Stock

Chop any kind of meat or chicken bones and put into a pan with water to cover. For each 600ml of water, add one onion, a few sticks of celery, a carrot and a bouquet garni. Bring to the boil then reduce heat, cover and simmer slowly for 2 to 4 hours, skimming occasionally. Cool completely (overnight in the fridge is best), then skim off the fat when it settles on the top. Strain stock and you are ready to make soup or a casserole. It can also be frozen before or after you make soup. Keep a supply of stock in the freezer for days when you are short on time or cannot be bothered cooking.

Basic Vegetable Stock

For a basic vegetable stock you can use any mixture of vegetables such as the outer leaves of cabbage, cauliflower stalks, outer celery stalks and leaves, green tops of leeks, onion peelings and any other vegetable trimmings available.

Chop them finely and add boiled water to barely cover. Add a bouquet garni, a few peppercorns and one or two cloves for flavour. Cover and boil for 20 to 30 minutes, then strain.

When time is tight, for a quicker, tastier alternative to commercial stock cubes try a long-life tetra pack of stock from the supermarket. These are available in salt-reduced varieties.

Soup freezes well, so make big batches and freeze in meal-sized portions. Great for a quick snack or lunch.

Low-fat and souper-delicious

- **EXTRA VEGETABLES** Add free vegetables (non starchy) to meet your vegetable quota easily. Try steaming or microwaving a combination before adding to a soup, or cooking them in the fat-free stock. Onion, carrot and celery is a good mix, as is capsicum, mushroom, snow peas and carrots.

- **MORE FLAVOUR** Add herbs and spices to your soups instead of salt. Try black or white pepper, oregano, parsley, garlic, ginger, basil, bay leaves, nutmeg or cloves.

- **THICK SOUP** If you prefer a thicker soup, add lots of vegetables, blend with a food processor and reheat.

- **TOMATO BASE** Instead of using stock, use tomato juice or puréed canned tomatoes as the base of a quick free soup. Add free vegetables and maybe a little stock, then blend.

- **CREAMED SOUP** Use skim or evaporated (canned) low-fat milk to make a creamy vegetable soup – with pumpkin, it works brilliantly.

- **CHILLED SOUP** In summer, chill soup for a refreshing change.

- **CUP OF SOUP** Make a cup of soup for less than 50 calories by adding free vegetables to a low-joule commercial packet soup. See the list in the *AHSG*.

- **GARNISH** Make soups more attractive with a sprinkling of finely chopped parsley, chives, shallots or mushrooms.

STOCK THE BLOCKS

■ Commercial stock cubes are high in salt, so freeze homemade stock in ice cube trays, transfer the cubes to a large plastic bag and use them as you need them. This way you can have small serves of low-salt homemade stock at your fingertips without resorting to stock cubes.

soups

Basic Chicken (or Beef) Stock
Makes 2 Litres

500g chicken or beef bones

1 large onion, roughly chopped

1 large carrot, roughly chopped

2 sticks celery, including the tops, diced

1 turnip, roughly chopped

2 litres cold water

6 black peppercorns

2 bay leaves

1 Put all of the ingredients into a large pot and slowly bring it to the boil.

2 Simmer the stock for 2 to 3 hours, removing any scum that rises to the surface.

3 Strain the stock and allow the liquid to cool.

4 Place in the refrigerator overnight. Remove any fat off the top the next day.

chOOz to lOOz Program
1 serve = Free

PER SERVE

KJ (cal)	50 (12)	Protein	0.3g
Fat	0.3g	Sodium	40mg
Saturated Fat	0.3g	Fibre	0g
Carbohydrate	2.3g		

Chicken or Beef Broth
Serves 8

2 litres Basic Chicken or Beef Stock (see recipe this page)

2 cups diced free vegetables

4 tablespoons fresh chopped parsley

1 Put the chicken or beef stock into a large pan and bring to the boil.

2 Add the diced vegetables and parsley. Simmer until the vegetables are soft.

chOOz to lOOz Program
1 serve = Free

PER SERVE

KJ (cal)	137 (33)	Protein	2.2g
Fat	0.6g	Sodium	40mg
Saturated Fat	0.2g	Fibre	1.7g
Carbohydrate	3.8g		

Quick Creamed Carrot Soup

Serves 8

4 chicken or beef stock cubes

5 cups boiling water

500g carrots, chopped

1 medium onion, chopped

1–2 bay leaves

½ cup skim milk

4 tablespoons chopped parsley

pepper to taste

1 Dissolve the stock cubes into the boiling water.

2 Add the chopped carrot, onion and bay leaves to the stock.

3 Simmer the soup in a large pot until the vegetables are tender.

4 Blend the mixture in a blender once cooked.

5 Reheat the soup mixture, bringing it to boiling point.

6 Allow the soup to cool slightly and then stir the skim milk through.

7 Serve garnished with parsley and pepper, to taste.

chOOz to lOOz Program
1 serve = Free

PER SERVE			
KJ (cal)	140 (33)	Protein	1.5g
Fat	0.3g	Sodium	420mg
Saturated Fat	0.1g	Fibre	2.0g
Carbohydrate	5.3g		

Pumpkin and Cauliflower Soup

Serves 4

500g pumpkin, peeled

1 large onion, chopped

1 cup chopped cauliflower

½ teaspoon curry powder

½ teaspoon cumin

1 tablespoon dried chives

2 cups chicken stock

1 Place the vegetables into a saucepan or casserole dish with all the other ingredients.

2 Cook until the vegetables are soft.

3 Purée in a blender for a smooth consistency. Reheat gently before serving.

chOOz to lOOz Program
1 serve = Free

PER SERVE INCLUDING VEGETABLE			
KJ (cal)	337 (81)	Protein	4.2g
Fat	0.9g	Sodium	624mg
Saturated Fat	0.5g	Fibre	2.7g
Carbohydrate	12.5g		

soups

Gazpacho
Serves 4

2 x 425g cans peeled tomatoes

1 medium onion

1 medium red capsicum, chopped

1 clove garlic

3 tablespoons lemon juice

½ cup chicken stock

few drops (1ml) Tabasco sauce

1 extra cup unsweetened tomato juice

1 Combine all the ingredients, except the tomato juice, in a blender and blend until smooth.

2 Add the tomato juice until the soup is at your desired consistency.

3 Chill before serving.

S

chOOz to lOOz Program
1 serve = Free

PER SERVE			
KJ (cal)	116 (28)	Protein	1.6g
Fat	0.3g	Sodium	449mg
Saturated Fat	0.1g	Fibre	1.5g
Carbohydrate	4.0g		

Beef, Basil and Tomato Soup
Serves 4

3 beef stock cubes

4 cups boiling water

500g canned peeled tomatoes

2 medium onions, diced

2 sticks celery, diced

basil to taste

pepper to taste

1 Dissolve the beef stock cubes into the 4 cups of boiling water.

2 Place all the ingredients including the stock, into a large pot, and simmer over a gentle heat until the vegetables are well cooked.

3 Place the soup into a blender and blend well. Reheat before serving.

S

chOOz to lOOz Program
1 serve = Free

PER SERVE			
KJ (cal)	215 (51)	Protein	2.2g
Fat	0.6g	Sodium	676mg
Saturated Fat	0.1g	Fibre	2.5g
Carbohydrate	7.9g		

Vegetable Minestrone
Serves 4

2 cups tomato juice, unsweetened

2 medium carrots, finely diced

4 cups water

2 cups shredded cabbage

2 cups diced zucchini

1 cup mushrooms, chopped

2 medium sticks of celery, chopped

1 clove garlic, crushed

1 bay leaf

2 tablespoons parsley, chopped

pepper to taste

1 Combine all ingredients except the parsley and pepper and gently simmer in a large pot until all the vegetables are tender.

2 Serve garnished with parsley and pepper.

S

chOOz to lOOz Program
1 serve = Free

PER SERVE			
KJ (cal)	271 (65)	Protein	3.5g
Fat	0.4g	Sodium	419mg
Saturated Fat	0g	Fibre	5.2g
Carbohydrate	7.6g		

Quick Cream of Asparagus Soup
Serves 2

1 chicken stock cube

1 cup boiling water

400g can asparagus tips

40ml light evaporated skim milk

salt and pepper to taste

4 tablespoons chopped parsley

1 Prepare the chicken stock by dissolving 1 chicken stock cube in the boiling water and stir well to ensure all the stock cube is dissolved.

2 Put the chicken stock and asparagus tips into a blender and blend until smooth.

3 Reheat the soup in a pan and stir through the light evaporated milk to add a creamier flavour. Season with salt and pepper.

4 Serve in a bowl garnished with parsley.

S

chOOz to lOOz Program
1 serve = 1 meat exchange

PER SERVE			
KJ (cal)	311 (74)	Protein	6.2g
Fat	0.5g	Sodium	510mg
Saturated Fat	0.1g	Fibre	8.3g
Carbohydrate	6.3g		

soups

Curried Zucchini Soup
Serves 2

1 onion, diced

canola or olive oil spray

2 zucchini, chopped

1 chicken stock cube

$1/8$ teaspoon curry powder

$2/3$ cup water

$2/3$ cup skim milk

1 Fry the onion until soft in a saucepan using spray oil.

2 Put the zucchini, chicken cube, onion, curry and water into a large pan and bring to the boil, reduce heat and simmer for 10 minutes until the vegetables are soft.

3 Slowly add the milk and simmer without boiling.

4 Transfer to a blender and blend until smooth. Reheat gently before serving.

S

chOOz to lOOz Program
1 serve = Free

PER SERVE			
KJ (cal)	282 (68)	Protein	5.3g
Fat	0.6g	Sodium	428mg
Saturated Fat	0.2g	Fibre	2.3g
Carbohydrate	9.2g		

Zucchini and Leek Soup
Serves 8

1 tablespoon olive oil

1 onion, finely chopped

2 leeks, washed and sliced

900g zucchini, grated

1.3 litres vegetable or chicken stock

4 short rosemary sprigs

1 Heat oil in a large pan. Add onion and leeks and cook for 5–10 minutes or until soft.

2 Add zucchini, and cook, stirring, for a further 5 minutes.

3 Add stock and the rosemary, bring to the boil.

4 Season, reduce heat and simmer for 20 minutes.

5 Cool soup slightly, remove rosemary stalks and blend the soup until smooth.

S

chOOz to lOOz Program
1 serve = Free

PER SERVE			
KJ (cal)	243 (58)	Protein	2.1g
Fat	2.9g	Sodium	802mg
Saturated Fat	0.5g	Fibre	2.6g
Carbohydrate	4.6g		

Artichoke and Leek Soup
Serves 6

1 onion, diced

2 leeks, chopped

1 large stick celery, diced

400g can artichokes, rinsed and drained

4 cups of Basic Chicken Stock (see page 56) or 3–4 chicken stock cubes in 4 cups boiling water

1 cup or 250ml skim milk

1 Sauté the onion, leeks and celery in a dash of water until tender, but not coloured.

2 Chop the artichokes and then add both the chicken stock and artichokes to the pan.

3 Pour stock onto the vegetables. Bring to the boil and cook for 30 minutes.

4 Allow the soup to cool and then purée in blender.

5 Return the soup to the pan, bring to boil and then return to simmer. Add the milk and stir well until combined.

***chOOz to lOOz* Program**

1 serve = Free

PER SERVE

KJ (cal)	259 (65)	Protein	4.9g
Fat	0.7g	Sodium	236mg
Saturated Fat	0.1g	Fibre	4g
Carbohydrate	7.1g		

soups

Creamy Celery and Onion Soup
Serves 8

4 chicken or beef stock cubes

5 cups of boiling water

500g celery, roughly chopped

2 medium onions, roughly chopped

1–2 bay leaves

½ cup skim milk

4 tablespoons chopped parsley

pepper to taste

1 Dissolve the stock cubes into the boiling water then add the chopped vegetables and bay leaves to the stock.

2 Simmer the soup in a large pot until the vegetables are tender then blend the mixture until smooth.

3 Reheat the soup mixture, bringing it to boiling point.

4 Allow the soup to cool slightly and then stir the skim milk through.

5 Serve garnished with parsley and pepper to taste.

chOOz to lOOz Program
1 serve = Free

PER SERVE			
KJ (cal)	116 (28)	Protein	1.6g
Fat	0.3g	Sodium	449mg
Saturated Fat	0.1g	Fibre	1.5g
Carbohydrate	4.0g		

Basic Lamb Stock
Serves 10

2 lamb shanks, all visible fat removed

1 bay leaf

6 black peppercorns

2 litres water

1 Put the lamb shanks, bay leaf, peppercorns and water in a large pan. Bring to the boil, reduce heat and simmer for approximately 1 to 1½ hours. Remove any scum that floats to the surface during cooking.

2 Allow the stock to cool and remove fat from the top. Strain before using.

Lamb and Brown Lentil Soup
Serves 10

½ cup raw brown lentils

2 litres Basic Lamb Stock (see this page)

2 medium onions, roughly chopped

2 medium carrots, chopped

3 sticks celery, chopped

½ teaspoon dried rosemary

2 medium potatoes, diced

1 Rinse the lentils under cold water, drain. Put the lentils and stock into a large pan. Bring to boil, reduce heat and simmer uncovered for 20 minutes.

2 Add the remaining ingredients and cook until the vegetables are tender.

---

chOOz to lOOz **Program**

1 serve = 1 meat exchange

PER SERVE

KJ (cal)	438 (104)	Protein	9.3g
Fat	2.9g	Sodium	47mg
Saturated Fat	1.2g	Fibre	2.5g
Carbohydrate	9.0g		

soups

Zucchini and Red Bean Soup
Serves 6

canola or olive oil cooking spray

4 zucchini, roughly chopped

2 carrots, roughly chopped

2 medium onions, diced

1 cup spinach leaves, chopped

500g fresh mushrooms, sliced

750g can red kidney beans, rinsed and drained

2 beef stock cubes

2½ cups water

fresh ground pepper

1 Lightly spray a large pan with cooking spray. Add the vegetables and cook over a medium heat for 2–3 minutes.

2 Add the kidney beans, stock cubes, water and pepper, bring to boil, reduce heat and simmer for 15 minutes.

3 Blend until smooth. Gently reheat before serving.

chOOz to lOOz Program
1 serve without bread = 2 meat exchanges

PER SERVE			
KJ (cal)	775 (185)	Protein	13.0g
Fat	1.4g	Sodium	676mg
Saturated Fat	0.2g	Fibre	12.5g
Carbohydrate	23.6g		

Pea Soup
Serves 4

3 beef stock cubes

3 cups boiling water

250g split peas, washed

1 large onion, chopped

2 large carrots, chopped

1 bay leaf

black pepper

1 Dissolve the beef stock cubes in the boiling water in a large pan.

2 Add the peas, onion, carrot, bay leaf and season with pepper. Bring to the boil, reduce heat and simmer for 1 hour or until the peas are soft.

chOOz to lOOz Program
1 serve without bread = 3 meat exchanges

PER SERVE			
KJ (cal)	955 (228)	Protein	15.7g
Fat	1.6g	Sodium	601mg
Saturated Fat	0.3g	Fibre	8.0g
Carbohydrate	34.3g		

Quick Potato and Onion Soup

Serves 4

2 chicken stock cubes

2 cups boiling water

1 cup skim milk

2 medium potatoes, cooked and mashed

1 medium onion, diced

2 teaspoons Worcestershire sauce

1 stick celery, chopped

1 tablespoon parsley, chopped

pepper to taste

1 To make the chicken stock, dissolve stock cubes in boiling water in a large pan.

2 Add the milk, potato, onion, Worcestershire sauce, celery and parsley. Bring to boil, reduce heat and simmer for 10 minutes or until the vegetables are soft.

3 Season to taste with pepper.

S

chOOz to lOOz **Program**
1 serve = 1 bread exchange

PER SERVE			
KJ (cal)	345 (83)	Protein	4.4g
Fat	0.3g	Sodium	688mg
Saturated Fat	0.2g	Fibre	1.6g
Carbohydrate	14.5g		

Sweet Potato and Leek Soup

Serves 4

500g sweet potato, peeled and sliced

2–3 medium leeks, chopped

15g fresh ginger, chopped

600ml water

black pepper

1 Put the sweet potato, leeks, ginger and water into a pan, bring to boil, reduce heat and simmer for 20 minutes or until the sweet potato is tender. Transfer the soup into a blender and blend until smooth.

2 The soup can be made to be a thinner consistency if required by the addition of more water.

chOOz to lOOz **Program**
1 serve without bread = 1 bread exchange

PER SERVE			
KJ (cal)	460 (110)	Protein	3.8g
Fat	0.4g	Sodium	24mg
Saturated Fat	0g	Fibre	4.3g
Carbohydrate	20.8g		

soups

Cream of Mushroom Soup
Serves 4

canola or olive oil spray

300g mushrooms, finely chopped

1 medium onion, finely chopped

2 tablespoons wholemeal flour

2 cups water

2 teaspoons powdered beef stock or
  1 beef stock cube

1 teaspoon prepared French mustard

375ml can light evaporated milk

freshly ground pepper

1 Spray a non-stick pan with oil and
  then fry the mushrooms and onions
  until the mushroom juices run.

2 Add the flour and cook for a further
  minute.

3 Gradually add the water, stirring
  constantly until smooth.

4 Add the stock and mustard, bring
  to boil, reduce heat and simmer for
  20 minutes.

5 Add the evaporated milk and
  cook for 5 minutes or until heated
  through. Season to taste.

chOOz to lOOz Program
1 serve without bread = 1 milk exchange

PER SERVE			
KJ (cal)	536 (128)	Protein	11.8g
Fat	0.9g	Sodium	484mg
Saturated Fat	0.3g	Fibre	2.9g
Carbohydrate	17.1g		

Chicken Noodle Soup
Serves 4

1 diced onion

1 clove garlic

2 sticks celery, julienned

2 large carrots (135g), julienned

6 cups Basic Chicken Stock
  (see page 56)

120g button mushrooms, thinly
  sliced

1 teaspoon grated ginger

100g dried rice vermicelli

2 spring onions

1 teaspoon soy sauce

1 Place all the ingredients into a
  pan and bring to the boil.

2 Cover, and reduce the heat to
  simmer.

3 Continue to simmer until all
  ingredients are cooked.

chOOz to lOOz Program
1 serve = 1 bread exchange

PER SERVE			
KJ (cal)	653 (156)	Protein	6.1g
Fat	1.2g	Sodium	158mg
Saturated Fat	0.2g	Fibre	4.2g
Carbohydrate	28.0g		

Hearty Minestrone
Serves 6

2 rashers rindless lean bacon, chopped

1 leek, trimmed, washed and sliced

1 onion, chopped

2 small potatoes, peeled and diced

2 carrots, diced

1 stick celery, sliced

1 litre Basic Beef Stock (see page 56)

½ teaspoon of dried basil

½ teaspoon dried oregano

2 x 425g cans diced tomatoes

1 tablespoon tomato paste

1 x 300g can red kidney beans

⅓ cup small shell or spiral dry pasta

½ cup green beans, sliced

¼ cup frozen peas

freshly ground black pepper, to taste

1 Cook the bacon, leek and onion in a large pan over a medium heat for 2 minutes or until browned.

2 Add the potatoes, carrots and celery. Cook, stirring for 1 minute.

3 Add the stock, tomatoes and tomato paste, bring to boil, reduce heat and simmer covered for 30 minutes.

4 Add green beans, kidney beans, pasta, peas and seasonings. Simmer for a further 10 minutes or until beans are soft and pasta is cooked.

S

chOOz to lOOz **Program**
1 serve = 2 meat exchanges and
1 bread exchange

PER SERVE			
KJ (cal)	970 (232)	Protein	12.8g
Fat	2.5g	Sodium	517mg
Saturated Fat	0.6g	Fibre	8.8g
Carbohydrate	34.5g		

All these recipes contain less than
1932KJ (462 calories) per serve.

Fish is a great healthy meal option: it is low in saturated fat and the Omega-3 fats that it does contain have numerous health benefits. Try to include fish or seafood in your diet at least twice a week.

fish & seafood

fish & seafood

Red Salmon and Vegetable Bake
Serves 4

1 tablespoon canola oil

1 large onion, chopped

210g can red salmon, drained

200g potatoes, cubed and cooked

2 slices wholemeal bread, crumbed

2 tablespoons chopped chives

2 tablespoons chopped parsley

1 teaspoon lemon pepper

1 egg, lightly beaten

½ cup skim milk

80g grated reduced-fat cheese

1 cup grated carrot

1 cup grated zucchini

1 Preheat oven to 180ºC. Heat the oil in a frying pan, add the onion and cook over a medium heat until golden. Remove from the pan and drain on absorbent paper.

2 Put the drained onion, salmon, potato, breadcrumbs, chives, parsley, lemon pepper, egg, milk, cheese, carrot and zucchini into a large bowl and mix well to combine.

3 Spoon the mixture into an ovenproof dish and bake for 30 minutes or until golden brown and set, and serve.

S C

chOOz to lOOz **Program**
1 serve = 3 meat exchanges, 2 fat exchanges and 1 bread exchange

PER SERVE			
KJ (cal)	1417 (339)	Protein	24.1g
Fat	17.6g	Sodium	749mg
Saturated Fat	5.6g	Fibre	4.0g
Carbohydrate	19.0g		

Salmon and Lemon Pepper Patties
Serves 4

210g can red salmon, drained

200g potatoes, cooked and mashed

2 slices wholemeal bread, crumbed

2 tablespoons chopped chives

2 tablespoons chopped parsley

lemon pepper to taste

2 tablespoons skim milk

1 egg, lightly beaten

1 tablespoons canola oil

1 Put the salmon, potatoes, breadcrumbs, chives, parsley, lemon pepper, milk and egg into a bowl and mix well to combine.

2 Divide the mixture into eight equal portions and shape into patties.

3 Heat the oil in a non-stick frypan, add the patties and cook for 8–10 minutes or until crisp and golden on both sides and warmed through.

4 Drain on absorbent paper before serving.

chOOz to lOOz Program
1 serve = 2 meat exchanges, ½ fat exchange and 1 bread exchange

PER SERVE			
KJ (cal)	1003 (240)	Protein	16.3g
Fat	12.7g	Sodium	590mg
Saturated Fat	2.5g	Fibre	2.0g
Carbohydrate	13.9g		

fish & seafood

Salmon Quiche
Serves 4

Pastry

160g wholemeal plain flour

40g canola margarine

Filling

4 eggs

1 cup evaporated skim milk

240g low-fat cottage cheese

4 spring onions, sliced

120g can red salmon, drained

1 tablespoon chopped fresh parsley

freshly ground black pepper to taste

40g reduced-fat tasty cheese, grated

1 Preheat oven to 200°C. Lightly grease a 24cm quiche dish with cooking spray.

2 Sift all but 1 tablespoon of the flour into a mixing bowl.

3 Rub the margarine into the flour until the mixture resembles fine breadcrumbs.

4 Add 1–2 tablespoons of iced water and mix to form a smooth dough. Do this on a lightly floured board until smooth.

5 Roll the dough on a lightly floured surface until it is large enough to cover the base and sides of the quiche dish. Fit the pastry into the dish. Trim the edges of the pastry to fit the dish and prick the pastry base with a fork. Line with baking paper and top with rice or baking beads. Bake for 15 minutes, or until the pastry is golden. Remove from oven, and discard baking papaer and rice. Reduce oven to 180°C.

6 Whisk together the eggs, evaporated milk and cottage cheese. Stir in the spring onions, salmon, parsley and pepper. Pour over the pastry base and sprinkle with the cheese. Bake for 45 minutes or until set.

C

chOOz to lOOz Program
1 serve = 2 meat exchanges,
2 bread exchanges,
1 milk exchange and 2 fat exchanges

PER SERVE			
KJ (cal)	1932 (462)	Protein	36.7g
Fat	19.3g	Sodium	503mg
Saturated Fat	5.5g	Fibre	4.6g
Carbohydrate	33.3g		

Prawn Chow Mein
Serves 2

1 large green capsicum

250g mushrooms

4 sticks celery

1 medium onion, chopped

375ml tomato juice

1 tablespoon soy sauce

1 teaspoon lemon juice

1 cup bean sprouts

400g peeled green prawns

150g broccoli florets, steamed

1 Thinly slice the capsicum, mushrooms and celery.

2 Lightly spray a non-stick frypan with cooking spray, add the onion and cook over a medium heat until browned.

3 Add the capsicum, mushroom and celery, tomato juice, soy sauce and lemon juice. Bring to the boil, reduce heat and simmer for 10 minutes.

4 Stir in the bean sprouts, prawns and broccoli and cook stirring for about 3 minutes or until the prawns are cooked.

S

chOOz to lOOz Program
1 serve = 3 meat exchanges

PER SERVE

KJ (cal)	1471 (340)	Protein	54.9g
Fat	2.1g	Sodium	2030mg
Saturated Fat	0.2g	Fibre	11.6g
Carbohydrate	18.2g		

fish & seafood

Fish Florentine
Serves 4

650g boneless fish fillets,
  such as whiting

½ cup water

½ cup lemon juice

3 sticks celery, finely chopped

1 bay leaf

4 shallots, finely chopped

500g English spinach leaves, washed,
  and roughly chopped

1 large tomato, thinly sliced

⅓ cup grated reduced-fat cheese

1 Preheat oven to 180°C. Place the fish,
  water, lemon juice, celery, bay leaf
  and shallots into a pan and simmer,
  covered, until the fish is tender.

2 Steam the spinach until tender,
  drain well.

3 Layer the spinach in the bottom of an
  ovenproof dish and place the steamed
  fish on top of the spinach, followed
  by the fresh tomato and finally the
  grated cheese. Bake for 5–10 until
  the cheese is melted and serve.

> **chOOz to lOOz Program**
> 1 serve = 3 meat exchanges

PER SERVE			
KJ (cal)	930 (223)	Protein	38.9g
Fat	4.0g	Sodium	247mg
Saturated Fat	1.8g	Fibre	4.6g
Carbohydrate	4.0g		

Fish Provençal
Serves 4

650g boneless fish fillets,
  such as whiting

⅓ cup lemon juice

¼ cup dry white wine

4 shallots, finely chopped

2 cloves garlic

¼ cup finely chopped parsley

2 medium tomatoes, chopped

pepper to taste

1 Place the fish fillets onto a baking
  tray lined with baking paper. Cook
  the fish under a preheated grill until
  tender. Drizzle some of the lemon
  juice to keep the fillets moist whilst
  cooking.

2 Put the white wine, shallots, garlic,
  parsley and tomatoes into a pan,
  bring to boil, reduce heat and
  simmer until the sauce thickens
  slightly.

3 Pour the sauce over the fish
  and serve.

> **chOOz to lOOz Program**
> 1 serve = 2.5 meat exchanges

PER SERVE			
KJ (cal)	735 (176)	Protein	33.4g
Fat	1.3g	Sodium	131mg
Saturated Fat	0.3g	Fibre	1.5g
Carbohydrate	3.0g		

Salmon and Vegetable Medley

Serves 4

250g can red salmon in brine

1 tablespoon canola oil

1 large onion, chopped

2 cloves garlic, crushed

1 medium capsicum, sliced

1 teaspoon curry powder

3 sticks celery, finely chopped

1 cup English spinach leaves, steamed, drained and roughly chopped

2 cups cooked brown rice

2 medium grated carrots, steamed

2 cups broccoli florets, steamed and chopped

2 hard-boiled eggs, chopped

1 tablespoon chopped parsley

1 tablespoon lemon juice

1 Drain the brine from the salmon and reserve the liquid. Flake the salmon and leave in a bowl.

2 Heat the oil in a non-stick frypan, add the onion, garlic, celery, capsicum and curry powder over a medium heat until the onion is soft.

3 Add the flaked salmon, rice, carrots, broccoli, eggs, parsley, lemon juice and reserved salmon liquid and cook until heated through.

PER SERVE			
KJ (cal)	1757 (420)	Protein	25.9g
Fat	13.1g	Sodium	463mg
Saturated Fat	2.6g	Fibre	8.6g
Carbohydrate	45.0g		

fish & seafood

Gourmet Tuna Rice Pie
Serves 8

1 tablespoon olive oil

1 onion, chopped

2 cloves garlic, crushed

1 red capsicum, chopped

100g mushrooms, diced

1 cup basmati or jasmine rice, rinsed

1¾ cups chicken stock

425g can tuna in brine, drained and flaked

125g 97% fat-free sun-dried tomatoes, drained, finely chopped

200g baby bocconcini cheese, drained and roughly chopped

50g parmesan cheese, finely grated

100g baby spinach leaves, shredded or frozen spinach, thawed

3 eggs, lightly beaten

1 Preheat oven to 190°C. Heat oil in a saucepan over medium heat. Add the onion and garlic and cook over a medium heat until golden. Add the capsicum and mushrooms and cook for 4 minutes.

2 Increase the heat to high and add the rice. Stir for 1 minute and stir in stock. Bring to a boil, reduce and simmer covered for 10 minutes. Remove from heat and allow to stand covered for 10 minutes.

3 Transfer rice mixture to a bowl and leave for 10 minutes to cool.

4 Grease and line the base of a 20cm springform pan with baking paper.

5 Add tuna, tomato, bocconcini, parmesan, spinach and egg to the cooled rice mixture and mix well to combine.

6 Place rice mixture into prepared pan. Bake for 40–50 minutes or until set and crisp around the edges. Stand in pan for a further 10 minutes then run a knife around the edges to loosen pie.

7 Cut pie into wedges and serve warm with salad.

S C

chOOz to lOOz Program
1 serve = 2 meat exchanges,
1 milk exchange, 1 bread exchange
and 1 fat exchange

PER SERVE			
KJ (cal)	1421 (340)	Protein	26.9g
Fat	12.4g	Sodium	691mg
Saturated Fat	5.4g	Fibre	3.6g
Carbohydrate	27.8g		

It's in the can

- **FISH FOR LUNCH** Use tuna or salmon in brine, water or tomato sauce in sandwiches and salads.

- **MAKE FISH PATTIES** Mix onion, egg, canned tuna, mashed pumpkin and/or potato, a little wholemeal flour or breadcrumbs and other finely grated vegetables such as carrots, and form into patties.

- **MOUTH-WATERING MORNAY** Add tuna or salmon to white sauce (recipe on page 131) to make a creamy mornay.

- **SALAD DAZE** Combine halved cherry tomatoes, steamed green beans, finely sliced red onion, chopped red capsicum and rocket leaves in a bowl. Top with tuna fillets in lemon pepper dressing.

- **NICE WITH RICE** Fold drained tuna in springwater through cooled cooked brown rice, corn kernels, chopped red capsicum, carrot, spring onions and lots of chopped dill and parsley. Dress with a generous squeeze of lime juice and a little extra virgin olive oil.

- **FISH FOR PASTA** Toss drained tuna in springwater through cooked penne or spaghetti, add grated lemon zest, lemon juice, chopped parsley, chilli, baby spinach, some grated parmesan cheese and a touch of extra virgin olive oil.

- **TIP-TOP TOAST** Spread a generous layer of hummus on toasted slices of wholegrain bread and top with torn basil leaves, sardines canned in tomato sauce and good sprinkle of freshly cracked black pepper.

- **OMEGA-3 SPREE** Roughly mash drained sardines in springwater with a big spoonful of natural yoghurt, chopped capers, finely chopped tomatoes and chopped fresh herbs. Use as a sandwich filling or on wholewheat crackers.

- **FISH PLUS EGGS** Fill an omelette with flaked smoked mackerel, chopped chives, spring onions and a little grated lemon zest.

- **HOLY MACKEREL** Canned mackerel adds a delightful flavour to a vegetable based soup. With herbs, spices and tomato paste, you have a quick, filling, nutritious fish and vegetable soup.

All these recipes contain less than
1964KJ (470 calories) per serve.

Lean meat is a delicious and easy
way to add protein to your diet.
The healthy options are endless.

meat

sauces

We love a bit of flavour and sauce on our meat but keeping the kilojoules and salt down can be a challenge.

THERE are plenty of flavour alternatives besides salt, fat and sugar. Add tang to sauces by using unsweetened, low-joule tomato sauce, pickles and chutneys. Spices such as cardamom, curry, cumin and nutmeg are great flavour enhancers for casseroles and stews. Some like it hot, so try chilli, pepper and paprika to add zest to dishes instead of resorting to shaking out too much salt.

Getting saucy

- **VALUE ADD** Use low-joule gravy as a base and add garlic and natural yoghurt for a Diane sauce, cracked pepper for a pepper sauce or sliced canned or fresh mushrooms for a mushroom sauce.

- **THICK AND FAST** Instead of using flour, try thickening sauces with mashed vegetables such as pumpkin or cauliflower.

- **MAKE IT CREAMY** Instead of using cream or sour cream, add plain non-fat yoghurt, low-fat evaporated milk or a small amount of low-fat sour cream to a sauce after cooking and heat gently before serving.

- **JUST CHILL** If using meat juices from a roast to make gravy, pour them into a cup and chill in the freezer for 15 minutes (if you are in a hurry) or in the fridge for a few hours. The fat will rise and solidify and is easily removed and discarded. Use the remaining juices for gravy, thickening with a little flour.

- **SALSA SAUCE** A jar of 97% fat-free salsa makes a quick and easy sauce. Just heat and serve over meat, chicken or fish. Choose a hot one if you like, or add chopped capsicum for a chunkier sauce.

Save time and use the jellied meat juices from last week's roast for this week's gravy.

marinades

Beware: many commercial marinade mixes are loaded with sugar, kilojoules and salt. Why not make your own?

MARINATING meat, chicken or fish, or cooking it in a mixture of the ingredients listed below will add loads of flavour without adding many kilojoules or much salt or fat. Marinating tenderises meat and keeps it moist while grilling, barbecuing or baking. Try these quick and easy ideas to make your own marinades. Make sure you have the ingredients in your pantry before you start.

Alternatively, you can buy commercial marinade mixes that are lower in salt, fat and sugar – consult the *AHSG*.

Marinate it

DIY (do-it-yourself) marinades are a healthy choice. Pick at least one ingredient from each column – then mix, marinate and enjoy.

BASE: Choose 1 or 2

- lemon juice
- vinegar
- dry wine
- tomato juice
- beef or chicken stock
- yoghurt
- puréed tomatoes
- tomato paste
- lime juice

ADD: Choose 1 or more

- soy sauce
- Worcestershire sauce
- Tabasco sauce
- mustard
- curry
- garlic
- paprika
- oyster sauce
- fish sauce
- teriyaki sauce

ADD: Choose 1 or more

- ginger
- shallots
- onion powder
- five spice powder
- herbs and spices such as coriander, basil, oregano, rosemary, tarragon, parsley, chilli
- lemongrass

meat

Beef Base
Serves 12

2 tablespoons olive oil

1½ kg lean beef chuck steak, chopped

3 large onions, chopped

3 cloves garlic, crushed

9 teaspoons wholemeal flour

3 beef stock cubes

900ml water

2 bay leaves

1 Heat 1 tablespoon of the oil in a large pan, add the beef in four batches and cook over a high heat until browned. Remove from the pan.

2 Heat remaining oil, reduce heat to medium, add the onions and garlic to the pan, cook for 5 minutes or until soft and browned.

3 Add the flour and cook until browned. Gradually add the combined stock cubes, water and bay leaves and cook, stirring until the sauce boils and mixture thickens.

4 Return the beef to the pan, bring to boil, reduce and simmer covered for 1½ hours or until the beef is tender. Remove the bay leaves when cooked.

TIMESAVING TIP
Separate Beef Base into three portions. Freeze two for future use. Use one to make Beef in Red Wine Sauce, one for Beef Casserole Diane Style and one for Spicy Mexican Casserole (see recipes following).

Beef in Red Wine Sauce
Serves 4

canola or olive oil cooking spray

2 medium carrots, chopped

½ cup dry red wine

1 bacon stock cube

500g button mushrooms, halved

⅓ of Beef Base recipe (see page 82)

2 teaspoons thyme, chopped

2 teaspoons basil leaves, chopped

2 tablespoons low-fat plain yoghurt

1 Spray a non-stick frypan with cooking spray, add the carrots and cook over a medium heat until soft.

2 Add the red wine and the crumbled stock cube, bring to boil, reduce heat and simmer until the liquid is reduced by half.

3 Stir in the mushrooms, Beef Base and herbs and simmer, covered for 10 minutes.

4 Remove the lid and simmer for 5 minutes or until the sauce thickens slightly.

5 Allow the dish to cool slightly and then stir through the yoghurt.

chOOz to lOOz Program
1 serve = 3 meat exchanges and ½ fat exchange. If served with ⅔ cup of cooked rice or 1 cup cooked pasta or 2 egg-size potatoes = 2 bread exchanges

PER SERVE

KJ (cal)	1230 (294)	Protein	32.7g
Fat	9.9g	Sodium	500mg
Saturated Fat	3.4g	Fibre	5.0g
Carbohydrate	10.4g		

meat

Beef Casserole Diane Style
Serves 4

1 dessertspoon olive oil

2 cloves garlic, crushed

500g button mushrooms, halved

400g can crushed tomatoes

2 tablespoons fresh parsley, chopped

2 tablespoons Worcestershire sauce

½ cup low-fat evaporated milk

1 teaspoon brandy

⅓ of Beef Base recipe (see page 82)

1 Heat the oil in a non-stick pan, add the garlic and cook until brown.

2 Add the mushrooms, crushed tomatoes, parsley, Worcestershire sauce, evaporated milk, brandy and bring to boil then reduce heat and simmer uncovered, until the sauce thickens.

3 Add the Beef Base and simmer for 10 minutes or until slightly thickened.

chOOz to lOOz **Program**
1 serve = 3 meat exchanges and
1 fat exchange. If served with ⅔ cup
of cooked rice or 1 cup cooked pasta, or
2 egg-size potatoes = 2 bread exchanges

PER SERVE			
KJ (cal)	1360 (326)	Protein	35.4g
Fat	12.1g	Sodium	509mg
Saturated Fat	3.5g	Fibre	5.8g
Carbohydrate	15.2g		

Fruity BBQ Sauce
Serves 6

canola or olive oil spray

¾ cup onion, finely chopped

50ml white wine vinegar

3 teaspoons mild French mustard

2 teaspoons Worcestershire sauce

8 peach halves, cooked or canned

120ml peach juice, no added sugar

½ cup tomato sauce, no added sugar

1 Lightly spray a non-stick pan with cooking spray. Add the onion and cook over a medium heat until golden.

2 Add the vinegar, mustard and Worcestershire sauce, cook, stirring for 3 minutes.

3 Add the peaches, peach juice and tomato sauce, bring to boil, reduce the heat and simmer for 15–20 minutes or until the mixture thickens. Serve with barbecued meats.

chOOz to lOOz **Program**
1 serve = ½ fruit exchange

PER SERVE			
KJ (cal)	166 (40)	Protein	1.0g
Fat	0.1g	Sodium	182mg
Saturated Fat	0g	Fibre	1.0g
Carbohydrate	8.0g		

Spicy Mexican Casserole
Serves 4

1 dessertspoon olive oil

2 cloves garlic, crushed

35g packet taco seasoning mix

2 teaspoons ground cumin

1 red capsicum, sliced

1 green capsicum, sliced

1 large white onion, diced

400g can crushed tomatoes

⅓ Beef Base recipe (see page 82)

2 tablespoons chopped fresh coriander

2 tablespoons fresh parsley, chopped

300g can red kidney beans, rinsed and drained

1 Heat the oil in a medium pan, add the garlic, seasoning mix and cumin and cook until fragrant.

2 Add the strips of capsicum and onion and cook over a medium heat until soft.

3 Add the crushed tomatoes, Beef Base, coriander, parsley and beans and simmer uncovered until thickened slightly.

S

chOOz to lOOz Program
1 serve = 3 meat exchanges, 1 bread exchange and 1 fat exchange.
If served with ⅔ cup of cooked rice or 1 cup cooked pasta or 2 egg-size potatoes = 2 bread exchanges

PER SERVE			
KJ (cal)	1629 (390)	Protein	35.4g
Fat	13.1g	Sodium	1569mg
Saturated Fat	3.6g	Fibre	9.2g
Carbohydrate	27.8g		

meat

Stuffed Red Capsicums
Serves 4

4 large red or green capsicums

1 teaspoon olive oil

1 medium onion, chopped

1 teaspoon garlic, crushed

500g lean beef mince

410g can crushed tomatoes

3 medium zucchini, halved and sliced

¼ cup tomato paste

1 teaspoon mixed dry herbs

1 teaspoon *Splenda*

½ cup grated parmesan cheese

1 Preheat the oven to 180°C.

2 Cut the capsicums lengthways through the stem, removing the ribs and seeds. Steam the capsicums over simmering water for 10 minutes to partly cook them.

3 Heat the oil in a pan, add the onions and cook over a medium heat until well browned.

4 Add the garlic and mince, stirring well to avoid any lumps.

5 Add the tomatoes, zucchini, tomato paste, herbs and *Splenda*, bring to boil, reduce the heat and simmer for 30 minutes.

6 Place the capsicums onto a tray and fill the capsicum halves with the sauce.

7 Sprinkle the stuffed capsicums with parmesan cheese and cook in the preheated oven for 20 minutes or until soft.

C

chOOz to lOOz Program
1 serve = 3 meat exchanges
and ½ milk exchange

PER SERVE			
KJ (cal)	1373 (328)	Protein	34.0g
Fat	14.0g	Sodium	410mg
Saturated Fat	6.0g	Fibre	5.0g
Carbohydrate	13.5g		

Beef Lasagne
Serves 6

canola or olive oil spray

1 medium onion, diced

2 cloves garlic, crushed

250g mushrooms, sliced

2 large carrots (135g), diced

2 medium zucchini, chopped

1 red capsicum, diced

425g can tomato soup

1 cup of fat-free Basic Beef Stock
(see page 56)

1 teaspoon dried basil

1 teaspoon dried oregano

360g low-fat beef mince

12 instant lasagne sheets

2 tablespoons chopped fresh parsley

White Sauce

1 tablespoon cornflour

250ml skim milk

80g reduced-fat cheddar cheese

1 tablespoon grated parmesan
cheese

1 Preheat oven to 180°C. Spray a
   non-stick pan with spray oil, add
   the onions and garlic, cook over a
   medium heat until browned. Add
   the remaining vegetables and cook
   until just browned.

2 Add the tomato soup, stock,
   herbs and mince. Stir well. Bring to
   the boil, reduce heat and simmer for
   30 minutes.

3 While the meat sauce is simmering,
   make the white sauce. Blend the
   cornflour with 2 tablespoons of
   milk to make a thick paste. Heat
   the remaining milk in a saucepan.
   Gradually add the cornflour paste to
   the skim milk, stirring constantly until
   the sauce boils and thickens. Add the
   cheese and cook until it melts.

4 Assemble the lasagne by starting
   with ⅓ of the meat sauce, top
   with lasagne sheets and ⅓ of
   the white sauce.

5 Continue layering until all of the
   ingredients are used. Finish with
   the cheese sauce. Sprinkle with
   a tablespoon of parmesan and
   chopped parsley.

6 Bake for 35–40 minutes or until
   the lasagne sheets are soft and
   the sauce is golden.

S

chOOz to lOOz Program
1 serve = 1 meat exchanges,
2 bread exchanges
and 1 milk exchange

PER SERVE			
KJ (cal)	1493 (357)	Protein	25.2g
Fat	8.4g	Sodium	795mg
Saturated Fat	4.0g	Fibre	5.4g
Carbohydrate	43.0g		

meat

Easy Beef Casserole
Serves 10

2 tablespoons olive oil

1.2 kg diced beef, chuck or blade steak

2 medium onions, cut into thick slices

2 leeks, white part only, sliced

2 cloves garlic, crushed,

3 sticks celery, cut into thick slices

2 large carrots, peeled, cut into thick slices

2 x 420g cans diced tomatoes

¼ cup red wine

1 cup Basic Beef Stock (see page 56)

1 Heat 1 tablespoon of oil in a large saucepan, add the beef in four batches, cook over a high heat until browned. Remove from the pan.

2 Reduce heat to medium, add remaining oil, onions, leeks, garlic, celery and carrot, cook for 5 minutes or until vegetables are soft.

3 Return the beef to pan with the tomatoes, wine and stock and bring to the boil. Reduce heat to low, simmer covered for 1 hour.

4 Uncover pan and simmer for 30 minutes, stirring occasionally until beef is tender.

chOOz to lOOz Program
serve = 3 meat exchanges
and 1 fat exchange

PER SERVE			
KJ (cal)	1151 (275)	Protein	35.6g
Fat	10.5g	Sodium	256mg
Saturated Fat	3.5g	Fibre	2.8g
Carbohydrate	6.9g		

Lamb Base
Serves 12

2 tablespoons olive oil

1½ kg lean lamb, diced

6 medium onions (300g)

3 cloves garlic, crushed

6 medium carrots (240g), sliced

6 sticks celery, chopped

6 bay leaves

3 beef stock cubes

1½ cups water

½ cup parsley, chopped

1 Heat 1 tablespoon of oil in a large fry pan. Add the diced lamb in four batches and cook over high heat, until browned.

2 Remove meat from pan. Heat the remaining oil, add the onions, garlic, carrots, celery and cook until soft and browned.

3 Stir in the lamb, bay leaves, crumbled stock cube, water and parsley, and bring to the boil. Reduce heat and simmer, covered for 1 hour or until the lamb is tender. Remove the bay leaves when cooked.

TIMESAVING TIP
Separate Lamb Base into three portions. Freeze two for future use. Use one to make Greek Lamb Casserole, one for Creamy Lamb Casserole with Vegetables and one for Lamb and Lentil Casserole (see recipes following).

meat

Greek Lamb Casserole
Serves 4

1 teaspoon olive oil

1 large onion, diced

2 large carrots, sliced

2 large red capsicums

750g can diced tomatoes

2 sprigs rosemary

2 tablespoons chopped fresh
 oregano

⅓ of Lamb Base recipe (see page 89)

2 cloves garlic, crushed

2 teaspoons lemon juice

1 Heat the oil in a large pan, add the
 onion and carrots and cook over a
 medium heat until browned.

2 While they are browning, halve the
 capsicums and remove the seeds,
 then place under a hot grill until the
 outer skins become blistered and
 black. Remove from the grill and
 allow to cool by placing them into
 a damp tea towel.

3 Once cooled, remove the skins and
 cut the flesh into strips.

4 Add capsicum, tomatoes, herbs and
 Lamb Base, bring to boil, reduce
 heat and simmer, uncovered until
 the sauce is thick. Stir in the garlic
 and lemon juice and serve.

---

chOOz to IOOz Program
1 serve = 3 meat exchanges and
1½ fat exchanges. If served with ⅔ cup
of cooked rice or 2 slices of bread
= 2 bread exchanges

PER SERVE

KJ (cal)	1503 (360)	Protein	32.2g
Fat	13.7g	Sodium	469mg
Saturated Fat	4.7g	Fibre	8.4g
Carbohydrate	22.4g		

Creamy Lamb Casserole with Vegetables
Serves 4

1 teaspoon olive oil

1 large onion, sliced

1 clove garlic, crushed

4 small potatoes, sliced

1 cup frozen peas

1 medium red capsicum, thinly sliced

1 tablespoon plain flour

¾ cup low-fat evaporated milk

⅓ of Lamb Base recipe (see page 89)

½ cup chopped parsley

1 Heat oil in a large pan and add the onion, garlic and potato, cook over a medium heat until the potatoes are tender.

2 Add the peas and capsicum, cooking until the capsicum is soft.

3 Add the flour and milk and cook stirring until the sauce boils and thickens slightly.

4 Add the Lamb Base and parsley and simmer uncovered for 10 minutes or until the sauce thickens slightly.

chOOz to lOOz Program
1 serve = 3 meat exchanges, 1 milk exchange, 1 bread exchange and ½ a fat exchange

PER SERVE

KJ (cal)	1757 (420)	Protein	37.4g
Fat	13.4g	Sodium	386mg
Saturated Fat	4.8g	Fibre	7.4g
Carbohydrate	33.4g		

meat

Lamb and Lentil Curry
Serves 4

1 teaspoon olive oil

2 cloves garlic, crushed

2 medium sweet potatoes, peeled and diced

2 large carrots (200g), sliced

2 teaspoons red curry paste (see *AHSG* for best brands)

¾ cup red lentils

2 cups water

2 beef stock cubes

⅓ of Lamb Base (see page 89)

2 tablespoons chopped fresh coriander leaves

1 Heat the oil in a large pan then add the garlic, sweet potato, carrots and curry paste and cook over a medium heat until browned and fragrant.

2 Add the lentils, water, crumbled stock cubes, and Lamb Base, bring to boil, reduce heat and simmer, covered for 15 minutes or until the lentils are tender.

3 Stir in the chopped coriander and serve.

S

chOOz to lOOz Program
1 serve = 3 meat exchanges,
1 fat exchange
and 2 bread exchanges

PER SERVE			
KJ (cal)	1964 (470)	Protein	39.5g
Fat	14.9g	Sodium	833mg
Saturated Fat	4.9g	Fibre	11.1g
Carbohydrate	39.7g		

Impossible Mediterranean Pie
Serves 4

1 tablespoon olive oil

1 onion, finely chopped

1 red capsicum, finely diced

2 medium zucchini, grated

60g lean ham, finely diced

3 eggs

1 cup skim milk

½ cup wholemeal self-raising flour

½ cup grated reduced-fat tasty cheese, grated

1 Preheat oven to 200°C. Grease a 4cm deep, 24cm base, ovenproof fluted ceramic quiche dish.

2 Heat oil in a non-stick frying pan over medium heat. Add onion and capsicum, cook over a medium heat for 4–5 minutes or until golden. Add the grated zucchini and diced ham and cook for a further 2 minutes. Remove from heat and cool.

3 Whisk the eggs, milk and flour in a bowl until combined. Stir in ham mixture and cheese.

4 Pour mixture into the quiche dish. Bake for 45–50 minutes or until set. Allow to stand for 10 minutes before serving.

S C

chOOz to lOOz Program
1 serve = 2 meat exchanges,
1 bread exchange, ½ milk exchange
and 1 fat exchange

PER SERVE			
KJ (cal)	1305KJ (312)	Protein	21.8g
Fat	16.7g	Sodium	635mg
Saturated fat	6.6g	Fibre	3.8g
Carbohydrate	17.3g		

meat

Vegetable Slice
Serves 4

2 large zucchini

2 large carrots

1 large onion

220g corn kernels

2 rashers lean bacon, finely chopped

4 eggs, lightly beaten

1 cup wholemeal self-raising flour

½ cup grated reduced-fat cheese

1 Preheat oven to 200ºC. Lightly grease a 20 x 30cm ovenproof dish. Coarsely grate the zucchini, carrots and onion (use a food processor if preferred).

2 Put the vegetables, bacon, eggs, flour and cheese into a bowl and mix to combine.

3 Pour the mixture into the prepared dish and bake for 1 hour or until set.

S

chOOz to lOOz Program
1 serve = 2 meat exchanges and
1 bread/starchy vegetable exchange

PER SERVE			
KJ (cal)	1063 (254)	Protein	17.1g
Fat	11.5 g	Sodium	616mg
Saturated Fat	3.8g	Fibre	4.7g
Carbohydrate	18.2g		

Simply Lite Bacon Zucchini Slice
Serves 4

3 rashers lean bacon, finely chopped

1 tablespoon olive oil

500g zucchini, coarsely grated

1 large onion, grated

4 eggs, lightly beaten

2 egg whites, lightly beaten

¼ cup water

1 carrot, grated

1 cup wholemeal self-raising flour

1 Preheat oven to 180ºC. Lightly grease a 20 x 30cm non-stick pan.

2 Put the bacon, olive oil, zucchini, onion, eggs, egg whites, water, carrot and self-raising flour into a bowl and mix well to combine.

3 Pour into the prepared tin and bake for 40 minutes or until set.

chOOz to lOOz Program
1 serve = 2 meat exchanges,
1 bread/starchy vegetable exchange
and 1 fat exchange

PER SERVE			
KJ (cal)	1040 (249)	Protein	15.9g
Fat	8.2 g	Sodium	498mg
Saturated Fat	3.1g	Fibre	6.4g
Carbohydrate	24.6g		

Crumbs!

Healthy cooking doesn't have to mean no more delicious schnitzel. Crumbed lean meat can be cooked with little fat using one of these three methods.

1 Spray crumbed meat on both sides with a little cooking oil and bake it on a rack in a hot oven.

2 Spray a frypan with non-stick spray or use a non-stick pan with half a teaspoon of oil heated in it. Fry schnitzel with the lid off until one side is brown and then remove. Add another half teaspoon of oil to the pan, turn the schnitzel over and brown the other side, again with the lid off. Once both sides are browned, turn the heat down, put the lid on the pan and cook slowly until the schnitzel is done all the way through. The lid helps keep the moisture in the pan, preventing the meat from drying out.

3 Brown the schnitzel as described above, then microwave to cook through and prevent drying out. This is the fastest method.

All these recipes contain less than
1930KJ (462 calories) per serve.

Skinned chicken or turkey breasts
are very low in fat and should
be used often. They are versatile,
tasty and very quick to cook.

chicken

chicken

Coriander Yoghurt Chicken
Serves 4

canola or olive oil cooking spray

4 skinless chicken breasts (720g)

500g low-fat plain yoghurt

2 teaspoons coriander, chopped

1 teaspoon cumin

1 teaspoon turmeric

1 lemon, juice and rind

1 Lightly spray a non-stick ovenproof dish with cooking spray. Trim all excess fat off the chicken and place into the prepared dish.

2 Put the yoghurt, spices and lemon rind into a bowl and mix to combine. Spread the spiced yoghurt over the chicken, pour the lemon juice over the chicken. Cover and allow the chicken to marinate in the refrigerator for several hours, or overnight.

3 Preheat oven to 180°C. Cover and bake the chicken for 20 minutes, baste the chicken with the marinade in the bottom of the pan. Bake uncovered for a further 10–15 minutes or until the chicken is tender.

chOOz to lOOz **Program**
1 serve = 3 meat exchanges
plus ½ milk exchange

PER SERVE

KJ (cal)	1339 (320)	Protein	46.2g
Fat	10.5g	Sodium	196mg
Saturated Fat	3.2g	Fibre	0.4g
Carbohydrate	8.1g		

Indian Chicken and Pumpkin Curry

Serves 4

1 tablespoon oil

4 small chicken breast fillets, cubed

1 medium onion, chopped

1 clove garlic, crushed

3 teaspoons curry powder

2 teaspoons paprika

1 teaspoon ground coriander

1 teaspoon ground cumin

½ teaspoon ground cloves

1 tablespoon cornflour

375ml low-fat evaporated milk

½ cup water

1 cup cooked pumpkin, peeled and diced

2 cups broccoli florets

1 Heat the oil in a pan, add the chicken and cook over a medium heat until browned.

2 Remove chicken, add the onions and garlic, cook for 2 minutes until softened.

3 Add the curry powder, paprika, coriander, cumin and cloves. Cook for 1 minute.

4 Blend the cornflour and 2 tablespoons of the water to form a thin paste, add the paste to the evaporated milk and remaining water and stir well.

5 Gradually add the cornflour and milk mixture to the saucepan stirring constantly until the sauce boils and thickens

6 Add the chicken, pumpkin and broccoli and simmer for 10 minutes.

---

chOOz to lOOz Program

1 serve = 3 meat exchanges plus
1 milk exchange and 1 fat exchange

PER SERVE

KJ (cal)	1854 (444)	Protein	52.5g
Fat	16.3g	Sodium	225mg
Saturated Fat	4.2g	Fibre	3.5g
Carbohydrate	20.0g		

chicken

Chicken and Mixed Vegetable Pie
Serves 5

Pastry

3 tablespoons canola oil (60ml)

¼ cup skim milk

1¼ cups wholemeal plain flour

Filling

2 medium carrots, sliced

1 medium sweet potato, peeled and diced

500g chicken breast fillets, chopped

1 cup frozen corn kernels, defrosted

1 cup frozen peas, defrosted

1 teaspoon dried rosemary

½ teaspoon white pepper

4 teaspoons wholemeal plain flour

1 cup chicken stock

1 Preheat oven to 200°C. Lightly spray a 20cm springform pan with oil.

2 To make the pastry, put the oil and milk into a bowl and mix to combine. Slowly add the flour, mix until a soft dough forms.

3 Make sure your hands are clean and cool. Roll the dough into a ball, flatten slightly and wrap in greaseproof paper. Chill for 15 minutes.

4 Bring a pan of water to boil, add the carrots and sweet potato. Boil, covered, over a medium heat until the vegetables are tender. Drain well.

5 Add the chicken, corn, peas, rosemary and pepper into a bowl and gently mix to combine.

6 Blend 2 tablespoons of the stock with 4 teaspoons of flour to form a smooth paste. Add the remaining stock and mix well. Add to the vegetable and chicken mixture. Spoon this mixture into the prepared tin.

7 Lightly flour a rolling pin and roll out the pastry on a lightly floured surface to a size that will cover your pie dish.

8 Place the pastry over the pie dish. Trim and decorate the edges. Cut two slits in the top of the pie to allow the steam to escape.

9 Bake in a preheated oven for 25–30 minutes or until golden brown.

---

chOOz to lOOz Program
1 serve = 3 meat exchanges, 2 bread exchanges plus 2 fat exchanges

PER SERVE

KJ (cal)	1930 (462)	Protein	30.1g
Fat	17.9g	Sodium	330mg
Saturated Fat	2.7g	Fibre	8.3g
Carbohydrate	40.6g		

Creamy Chicken Parcels with Chive Sauce

Serves 4

Sauce

375ml low-fat evaporated milk

2 tablespoons chives

½ teaspoon tarragon

½ teaspoon powdered chicken stock

4 teaspoons cornflour

Chicken Dish

4 sheets filo pastry

1 teaspoon safflower or canola oil

4 small skinless chicken breasts fillets (720g)

½ teaspoon tarragon

juice of 1 lemon

2 teaspoons parsley, chopped

60ml skim milk

rind of 1 lemon

1 Preheat oven to 200ºC. Fold each sheet of filo pastry in half and place onto a lightly sprayed baking tray.

2 Heat the oil in a frypan, add the chicken breasts and cook over a medium heat until browned on both sides.

3 Place one chicken breast onto the centre of each sheet of filo pastry.

4 Sprinkle the chicken breast with the tarragon and lemon juice.

5 Fold the pastry over the chicken breast to form a parcel, and brush the parcel with the skim milk. Place the parcels onto a non-stick baking tray.

6 Bake for 10–15 minutes or until golden brown and the chicken is tender.

7 To make the sauce, heat the milk in a saucepan over a low heat. Add the herbs and stock.

8 Blend the cornflour with 1 tablespoon of water to form a smooth paste. Gradually add to the milk and cook stirring until the mixture boils and thickens.

9 Serve the parcels topped with the sauce and sprinkle with the parsley and lemon rind.

chOOz to lOOz Program

1 serve = 3 meat exchanges, 1 bread exchange plus 1 milk exchange

PER SERVE

KJ (cal)	1627 (389)	Protein	40.5g
Fat	11.8g	Sodium	403mg
Saturated Fat	3.5g	Fibre	0.5g
Carbohydrate	21.8g		

chicken

Chicken and Mixed Vegetable Hotpot
Serves 4

canola or olive oil cooking spray

400g chicken breast fillets, diced

2 onions, sliced into rings

2 carrots, sliced

$^2/_3$ cup water

1 chicken stock cube

½ teaspoon dried sage

½ teaspoon mustard powder

2 potatoes, peeled, thinly sliced

1 tablespoon cornflour

3 tablespoons water (extra)

1 Lightly spray a large fry pan with cooking spray, add the chicken and cook for 5 minutes, or until brown, remove.

2 Lightly spray the pan again with cooking spray, add the onions and cook for 5 minutes, or until golden brown. Add the carrots, water, crumbled stock cube, sage and mustard and bring to the boil. Reduce heat to a simmer, cover and cook for 15 minutes, stirring occasionally.

3 Add the potato and chicken and simmer, covered for around 25 minutes, or until potato is cooked.

4 Blend the cornflour and 3 tablespoons of water until a smooth paste is formed.

5 Add the cornflour mix to the pan and cook stirring for 5 minutes until the sauce boils and thickens.

chOOz to lOOz Program
1 serve = 2 meat exchanges and 1 bread exchange

PER SERVE			
KJ (cal)	898 (215)	Protein	24.0g
Fat	5.8g	Sodium	279mg
Saturated Fat	1.8g	Fibre	2.6g
Carbohydrate	15.0g		

Mushroom and Chicken Loaf

Serves 4

1 cup wholemeal breadcrumbs

½ cup low-fat evaporated milk

500g lean chicken mince

250g mushrooms, sliced

1 medium onion, chopped

½ cup chopped parsley

1 egg, lightly beaten

2 tablespoons sweet chilli sauce

2 medium carrots, grated

canola or olive oil spray

1 Pre heat oven to 180°C. Grease and line a 14cm x 21cm loaf tin.

2 Put the breadcrumbs, milk, mince, mushrooms, onion, parsley, egg, sweet chilli sauce and carrots into a bowl and mix well to combine.

3 Turn the mixture into the prepared loaf tin. Bake for 30 minutes or until juices run clear when tested with a skewer.

---

chOOz to lOOz Program
1 serve = 3 meat exchanges, plus
1 bread exchange and 1 milk exchange

PER SERVE

KJ (cal)	1562 (374)	Protein	38.3g
Fat	9.9g	Sodium	498mg
Saturated Fat	2.9g	Fibre	4.9g
Carbohydrate	30.0g		

chicken

Chicken Stroganoff
Serves 4

1 teaspoon canola oil

500g chicken breast fillets, thinly sliced

2 medium onions, sliced

1 tablespoon wholemeal plain flour

½ cup chicken stock

2 tablespoons tomato paste

½ teaspoon thyme

1 bay leaf

1 cup mushrooms, sliced

1 medium red capsicum, thinly sliced

2 medium carrots, halved and thinly sliced

1 cup broccoli florets

½ cup *Carnation* skim milk powder, mixed with ½ cup water

1 Heat the oil in a pan, add the chicken and onions and cook over a medium heat until the chicken is browned.

2 Add the flour and cook stirring for 1 minute.

3 Gradually add half of the stock to the pan, stirring well, to form a smooth paste. Slowly add the rest of the stock, stirring constantly until the sauce boils and thickens,

4 Add the tomato paste, herbs, mushrooms, capsicum, carrots, broccoli, and skim milk mixture, bring to boil, reduce heat and simmer for 30–45 minutes or until the chicken is tender.

chOOz to lOOz Program
1 serve = 3 meat exchanges

PER SERVE			
KJ (cal)	1191 (285)	Protein	35.0g
Fat	8.5g	Sodium	375mg
Saturated Fat	2.3g	Fibre	3.8g
Carbohydrate	15.2g		

Chicken Cacciatore
Serves 4

700g chicken breast

2 tablespoons cornflour

canola or olive oil cooking spray

1 onion, chopped

2 cloves garlic, chopped

3 medium carrots, sliced

250g mushrooms, sliced

3 sticks celery, sliced

3 medium zucchini, sliced

3 tablespoons tomato paste

1 chicken stock cube

2 cups water

2 medium onions, sliced

½ cup low-fat evaporated milk

1 Coat the chicken fillets in cornflour, shake off any excess.

2 Spray a non-stick pan with cooking spray, add the chicken and cook over a medium heat until browned. Remove from the pan.

3 Re-spray the pan with oil, add the onions, garlic and 2 tablespoons of water and cook until softened.

4 Add the chicken, carrots, mushrooms, celery, zucchini, tomato paste, stock cube and water, bring to boil, reduce heat and simmer covered for 1 hour. Remove the lid and simmer uncovered for 5–10 minutes or until the sauce thickens slightly.

5 Once the dish is cooked, turn off the heat and stir through the evaporated milk.

chOOz to lOOz Program
1 serve = 3 meat exchanges

PER SERVE			
KJ (cal)	1368 (327)	Protein	44.5g
Fat	10.4g	Sodium	484mg
Saturated Fat	3.1g	Fibre	5.6g
Carbohydrate	10.9g		

chicken

Cornish Chicken and Corn Pasties
Makes 12

Pastry

125g canola margarine, well chilled

3 cups (420g) wholemeal self-raising flour

½ cup low-fat ricotta cheese

¾ cup iced water

Filling

2 (200g) medium potatoes, finely chopped

1 (150g) medium turnip, finely chopped

1 (75g) small carrot, finely chopped

3 sticks celery

¼ cup corn kernels, drained

2 medium onions, finely chopped

300g lean chicken mince

2 teaspoons dried thyme

freshly ground pepper, to taste

1 Preheat oven to 180°C. Place the potato, turnip, carrot, celery, corn, onions, chicken mince, thyme and pepper into a food processor. Process until diced.

2 To prepare the pastry, cut the well-chilled margarine into the wholemeal flour until the mixture resembles fine breadcrumbs. Add the ricotta and cut in to resemble fine breadcrumbs.

3 Gently add the iced water and mix with a fork until the mixture comes together. Gather the mixture into a smooth ball. Roll out the pastry on a lightly floured surface. Cut out 12 circles of 17cm diameter.

4 Place ⅓ cup of the pastie filling into the centre of the pastry circle. Lightly brush the edges with water. Fold over the pastie to enclose the filling. Cut 2 small slits in the top of the pastie for the steam.

5 Use a fork to decorate the edges of the pastie. Place the pasties on a baking tray and bake for 20–25 minutes or until golden brown.

chOOz to lOOz Program
1 serve = 1 meat exchange, 2 bread exchanges and 2 fat exchanges

PER SERVE			
KJ (cal)	1169 (280)	Protein	11.0g
Fat	12.5g	Sodium	327mg
Saturated Fat	2.7g	Fibre	5.0g
Carbohydrate	28.0g		

Lemon and Ginger Chicken
Serves 2

2 medium skinless chicken
  breasts fillets

2 tablespoons cornflour

Sauce

½ cup lemon juice

1–1½ tablespoons cornflour

2 chicken stock cubes

1–2 teaspoons grated ginger

1 tablespoon *Splenda*

1 Preheat oven for 150ºC. Coat the
  chicken in the cornflour, shake off
  any excess. Put the chicken on to a
  non-stick baking tray and bake for
  20–30 minutes or until the chicken
  is tender.

2 To make the sauce, blend
  2 tablespoons lemon juice with
  the cornflour to make a smooth
  paste. Add the crumbled stock
  cubes, ginger, *Splenda* and
  remaining lemon juice.

3 Cook the sauce over a medium heat,
  stirring constantly until the sauce
  boils and thickens.

4 Pour the sauce over the chicken and
  bake for a further 5 minutes.

S

chOOz to lOOz **Program**
1 serve = 3 meat exchanges and
1 bread exchange

PER SERVE			
KJ (cal)	1427 (341)	Protein	38.5g
Fat	10.3g	Sodium	876mg
Saturated Fat	3.2g	Fibre	0.3g
Carbohydrate	21.5g		

All these recipes contain less than
2044KJ (489 calories) per serve.

Choosing a vegetarian evening
meal once or twice a week
is good for your health,
wallet and the environment.
Reducing meat from the diet
requires you to obtain protein
from other sources, such as
legumes and dairy foods.

vegetarian

vegetarian

Asparagus and Sesame Stir-fry
Serves 4

2 teaspoons sesame oil

2 teaspoons olive oil

1 medium onion, chopped

2 cloves garlic, chopped

2 teaspoons grated ginger

2 medium red or green capsicums, sliced

1 bunch asparagus, sliced (or 425g tinned)

800g firm tofu, cubed

500g mushrooms, sliced

1 dessertspoon sesame seeds

2 tablespoons soy sauce

2 teaspoons honey

1 Heat the oils in a pan or wok, add the onion and garlic and stir-fry over a medium heat until golden.

2 Add the grated ginger, capsicum, asparagus, mushrooms, tofu and sesame seeds. Stir-fry mixture for 3–5 minutes or until the vegetables are tender.

3 Add the combined soy sauce and honey and cook until heated through.

S

chOOz to lOOz **Program**
1 serve = 3 meat exchanges and 1 fat exchange

PER SERVE			
KJ (cal)	1590 (380)	Protein	32.4g
Fat	19.6g	Sodium	951mg
Saturated Fat	2.8g	Fibre	12.1g
Carbohydrate	12.6g		

Pumpkin and Lentil Curry

Serves 4

425g can crushed tomatoes

140g tomato paste

1 teaspoon curry powder

1 teaspoon cumin

2 teaspoons coriander, chopped

½ teaspoon garam masala

400g firm tofu

500g chopped peeled pumpkin

1 cup diced carrots

1 cup chopped green beans

1 cup broccoli florets

1 cup spinach leaves

1 dessertspoon olive oil

2 medium onions, chopped

2 cloves garlic, crushed

360g cooked lentils (1⅓ cups)

TIMESAVING TIP

You don't have to soak lentils before cooking – just add directly to soups and stews. They are a very convenient legume because they take only 20–30 minutes to cook.

1 Put the tomatoes, tomato paste, mild curry powder, cumin, coriander and garam masala into a bowl and mix to combine.

2 Cut the tofu into cubes and marinate the tofu in the tomato spice mixture for several hours or overnight.

3 Steam the pumpkin, carrots, green beans, broccoli and spinach until just tender. Put aside and allow to cool.

4 Heat the oil in the pan, add the onions and garlic and cook over medium heat until golden.

5 Add the cooked lentils, tofu, remaining marinade and steamed vegetables.

6 Bring the mixture to the boil, reduce the heat, simmer covered for 5 minutes or until heated through.

chOOz to lOOz Program

1 serve = 3 meat exchanges and ½ fat exchange

PER SERVE			
KJ (cal)	1205 (288)	Protein	22.6g
Fat	10.3g	Sodium	329mg
Saturated Fat	1.4g	Fibre	11.2g
Carbohydrate	20.8g		

vegetarian

Spinach and Mushroom Lasagne
Serves 4

canola or olive oil cooking spray

2 onions, chopped

1 clove garlic

250g frozen spinach

240g smooth low-fat ricotta cheese

1/4 teaspoon ground nutmeg

810g can chopped tomatoes

3 tablespoons tomato paste

pepper to taste

1 teaspoon dried basil

1/2 teaspoon dried oregano leaves

2 cups mushrooms, sliced and steamed

1 tablespoon plain flour

1 1/2 cups skim milk

240g instant wholemeal lasagne sheets

120g light mozzarella cheese

1 Preheat the oven to 180°C.

2 Lightly spray a pan with cooking spray, cook the onions and garlic until soft.

3 Put the spinach, ricotta cheese and nutmeg into a bowl and mix to combine.

4 Put the tomatoes, tomato paste, pepper, herbs and mushrooms into a separate bowl and combine.

5 Add half the onion mixture to the spinach bowl and half to the tomatoes.

6 Blend the flour and 3 tablespoons of milk to form a smooth paste. Add the remaining milk to a saucepan and heat until warm.

7 Gradually add the flour mixture, stirring constantly until the sauce boils and thickens. Stir in the mushrooms.

8 Line the base of an ovenproof dish, 6cm deep, 18cm x 24cm with one quarter of the lasagne sheets, leave gaps to allow for expansion. Top with half of the tomato mixture.

9 Place another layer of lasagne on top, followed by the spinach mixture, then more lasagne sheets, and the remaining tomato mixture.

10 Finish with a layer of lasagne sheets and the white sauce, sprinkle with the mozzarella. Bake for 1 hour or until golden.

(C)

chOOz to lOOz Program
1 serve = 3 meat exchanges,
1 milk exchange, 2 bread exchanges
and 1 fat exchange

PER SERVE			
KJ (cal)	2044 (489)	Protein	32.2g
Fat	12.8g	Sodium	482mg
Saturated Fat	7.1g	Fibre	11.8g
Carbohydrate	54.8g	Iron	6.1mg

Spinach and Cheese Cannelloni

Serves 4

12 cannelloni shells

Filling

250g frozen spinach, thawed

225g low-fat ricotta cheese

1 pinch nutmeg

1 egg

Sauce

olive oil or canola cooking spray

1 medium onion, finely chopped

1 clove garlic, crushed

420g can tomato soup

1 tsp ground basil, dried

½ cup water

ground black pepper

Topping

120g reduced-fat cheese, grated

1 Preheat oven to 200°C. Put the spinach, ricotta, nutmeg and egg into a bowl and mix to combine.

2 Fill the cannelloni shells with the spinach mixture.

3 To make the sauce, lightly spray a non-stick pan with cooking spray, add the onion and garlic and cook over a medium heat until browned. Add the tomato soup, dried basil and water, bring to boil, reduce heat and simmer for 10 minutes or until the sauce thickens slightly.

4 Pour half the sauce over the base of a greased baking dish. Top with a layer of filled cannelloni shells. Cover the shells with the remaining sauce and sprinkle with the grated cheese. Bake for 25–30 minutes or until the shells are soft and the topping is golden brown.

S **C**

çhOOz to lOOz Program
1 serve = 2 meat exchanges,
2 bread exchanges
and 2 fat exchanges

PER SERVE			
KJ (cal)	1517 (363)	Protein	22.3g
Fat	14.2g	Sodium	995mg
Saturated Fat	8.1g	Fibre	5.1g
Carbohydrate	34.3g		

vegetarian

Red Bean Casserole

Serves 6

1 tablespoon olive oil

500g baby onions

2 cloves garlic, crushed

360g can red kidney beans, rinsed and drained

3 carrots, chopped

1 cup vegetable stock

1½ cups red wine

¼ cup tomato paste

2 zucchini, chopped

500g frozen broad beans

2 tablespoons fresh rosemary

1 tablespoon Worcestershire sauce

2 tablespoons cornflour

¼ cup water

1 Preheat oven to 180ºC. Heat the oil in a large flame proof casserole dish on stove top. Add the onions, garlic, kidney beans and carrots. Cook, stirring, until the onions are browned.

2 Add the stock, wine, tomato paste and zucchini to the mixture and bring to the boil, whilst stirring.

3 Bake for about 30 minutes then return the casserole to the stove top.

4 Meanwhile peel the broad beans, add the beans, rosemary and Worcestershire sauce.

5 Blend the cornflour and water in a bowl to form a smooth paste.

6 Gradually add the cornflour mixture to the casserole, stirring constantly until the sauce boils and thickens. Simmer for 5 minutes.

---

chOOz to lOOz Program
1 serve = 2 meat exchanges
and 1 fat exchange

PER SERVE

KJ (cal)	1077 (258)	Protein	12.4g
Fat	4.2g	Sodium	493mg
Saturated Fat	0.6g	Fibre	12.4g
Carbohydrate	26.9g		

Tofu Patties
Makes 10 patties

2 teaspoons sunflower oil

1 small onion, finely chopped

1 stick celery, finely chopped

½ red capsicum, finely chopped

500g firm tofu

1 egg, beaten

2 tablespoons wholemeal plain flour

2 tablespoons tamari or soy sauce

2 teaspoons curry powder

2 tablespoons polenta

olive oil or canola cooking spray

1 Preheat oven to 180°C.

2 Heat 1 teaspoon of the oil in a frypan, add the onion, celery and capsicum and cook over medium heat until soft.

3 Strain the tofu and blend or mash with a fork. Add the egg, flour and soy sauce and mix well to combine.

4 Add the cooked vegetables and curry powder.

5 Form into small patties, coat in the polenta, shaking off any excess.

6 Lightly oil tray with the remaining oil. Place patties onto the tray and spray lightly with spray oil and bake for 20–25 minutes or until brown.

chOOz to lOOz **Program**
1 serve = 1 meat exchange
and 1 fat exchange

PER SERVE			
KJ (cal)	403 (96)	Protein	7.5g
Fat	4.9g	Sodium	284mg
Saturated Fat	0.8g	Fibre	1.7g
Carbohydrate	4.6g		

vegetarian

Cheesey Spinach and Corn Pie
Serves 6

Pastry

1 cup plain wholemeal flour

150g low-fat cottage or
ricotta cheese

Filling

3 eggs

1 cup low-fat evaporated milk

100g low-fat cottage cheese

425g can corn kernels

1 medium onion, diced

250 g frozen spinach, thawed

ground black pepper

1 Preheat oven to 200°C. Lightly grease the base and sides of a 20cm springform pan with cooking spray.

2 To make the pastry, put the flour and cottage cheese into a bowl and mix to form a smooth pastry. Press firmly into a pie dish, refrigerate for 30 minutes.

3 Beat the eggs, add the milk, cottage cheese, corn, onion, spinach and pepper and mix well to combine.

4 Pour over the base and cook for 40–45 minutes or until pastry is golden.

chOOz to lOOz **Program**
1 serve = 2 bread exchanges,
1 milk exchange
and 1 fat exchange

PER SERVE

KJ (cal)	1154 (276)	Protein	20.7g
Fat	4.6g	Sodium	366mg
Saturated Fat	1.3g	Fibre	7.0g
Carbohydrate	34.4g		

Lentil Patties
Serves 4

1 cup cooked and drained lentils or drained canned lentils

½ cup mashed pumpkin

½ cup mashed potato

1 onion, finely chopped

½ cup rolled oats

¼ cup breadcrumbs

½ teaspoon ground cumin

½ teaspoon ground coriander

chilli powder and ground black pepper, to taste

2 tablespoons parsley, finely chopped

2 tablespoons lemon Juice

extra breadcrumbs

canola or olive oil cooking spray

1 Put the lentils and remaining ingredients, except the breadcrumbs, into a bowl and mix to combine. Divide the mixture into four and shape into patties.

2 Roll in breadcrumbs, shaking off any excess.

3 Lightly spray the patties with cooking spray and place on a non-stick baking tray.

4 Cook under a preheated grill on medium until browned on each side and heated through. If necessary, remove from grill during cooking and spray each side lightly with non-stick spray oil.

chOOz to lOOz Program
1 serve = 1 meat exchange and 2 bread exchanges

PER SERVE			
KJ (cal)	923 (221)	Protein	10.4g
Fat	2.3g	Sodium	169mg
Saturated Fat	0.5g	Fibre	5.4g
Carbohydrate	36.3g		

vegetarian

Easy Tomato and Vegetable Pasta Sauce
Serves 4

1 large red onion, diced

2 medium zucchini, diced

2 red capsicums, diced

420g can tomatoes, diced

2 cups mushrooms, diced

2 teaspoons dried Italian herbs

4 teaspoons minced garlic

2 tablespoons tomato paste

2 teaspoons olive oil

1 dessertspoon seeded mustard

3 dessertspoons balsamic vinegar

1 vegetable stock cube

½ cup water

1 Add oil to large saucepan and heat until hot. Reduce heat to medium, then add garlic and onion and stir for a few minutes until onion is browned.

2 Add capsicum, then zucchini, then mushrooms in around two minute intervals, while stirring regularly.

3 Lastly, add tomatoes and balsamic vinegar and stir to combine.

4 Mix mustard, tomato paste, herbs, stock cube and water together separately in a bowl, then add to the saucepan, stir and bring to the boil.

5 Reduce heat and simmer for at least 30 minutes, or until vegetables are cooked through and sauce is thick.

---

chOOz to lOOz Program
1 serve = ½ fat exchange

PER SERVE			
KJ (cal)	476 (113)	Protein	5g
Fat	3.3g	Sodium	377mg
Saturated Fat	0.5g	Fibre	5.2g
Carbohydrate	12.8g		

Roast Vegetable Pasta
Serves 6

500g cherry tomatoes, halved

250g pumpkin, diced

250g mushrooms, diced

2/3 cup balsamic vinegar

2 tablespoons brown sugar

200g dry fettuccine or 400g fresh
  fettuccine

200g baby spinach leaves or
  200g frozen spinach, thawed

2 tablespoons basil pesto

120g low-fat feta cheese, crumbled

40g shaved parmesan cheese

1 Preheat oven to 200°C. Place
  tomatoes, pumpkin and mushrooms
  in a roasting pan.

2 Put the vinegar and sugar into a
  bowl and mix to dissolve the sugar,
  pour over vegetables.

3 Roast for 25–30 minutes or
  until vegetables are soft, stir
  the vegetables a couple of
  times during cooking.

4 Meanwhile, cook pasta in a large
  saucepan of boiling, salted water,
  until al dente. Drain and return the
  pasta to pan.

5 Add spinach, pesto and feta and
  toss gently over low heat until just
  combined.

6 Divide pasta between serving bowls,
  spoon over the roast vegetables and
  any juice.

7 Top with parmesan and serve.

chOOz to lOOz Program
1 serve = 2 bread exchanges,
1 meat exchange, 1 milk exchange
and 1 fat exchange

PER SERVE

KJ (cal)	1187 (283)	Protein	15.6g
Fat	8.5g	Sodium	400mg
Saturated Fat	4.0g	Fibre	5.0g
Carbohydrate	32g		

All these recipes contain less than 1050KJ (250 calories) per serve. The Asian Beef Salad and the Thai Beef Salad are considered main meals.

They are a vital part of a healthy diet, but sometimes it can be hard to make vegetables interesting. Experiment with what's in season, and mix and match colours for the best flavour and most nutrition, with very few kilojoules. Enhance the fresh flavours with light sauces and dressings.

vegetables & salads

vegetables & salads

Devilled Carrots
Serves 4

400g carrots, peeled and diced

½ teaspoon prepared mustard

5 drops Tabasco sauce

5 drops Worcestershire sauce

pepper to taste

paprika to taste

chopped parsley, to garnish

1 Place the carrots in boiling water or steamer and cook for 10 minutes until soft, drain.

2 Mix the mustard, Tabasco sauce, Worcestershire sauce, pepper and paprika to taste.

3 Add the sauce to the carrots, mix to coat the carrots in the sauce, garnish with parsley.

chOOz to lOOz Program
1 serve = Free

PER SERVE

KJ (cal)	152 (36)	Protein	1.0g
Fat	0.3g	Sodium	55mg
Saturated Fat	0g	Fibre	2.9g
Carbohydrate	6.1g		

Zucchini and Tomato Crumble
Serves 4

olive oil spray

2 onions, finely chopped

2 cloves garlic, crushed

2 zucchini, cut into thick slices

4 medium tomatoes, chopped

¼ cup parsley, finely chopped

1 tablespoon breadcrumbs

60g reduced-fat cheddar cheese, grated

1 Lightly spray a pan with olive oil spray, add the onions, garlic and zucchini and cook over a medium heat until soft.

2 Add the tomatoes and parsley and cook for a further 2–3 minutes.

3 Spoon the tomato mixture into an ovenproof baking dish, sprinkle with the breadcrumbs and cheese and bake in the oven until the cheese is melted.

chOOz to lOOz Program
1 serve = ½ milk exchange

PER SERVE

KJ (cal)	466 (112)	Protein	7.8g
Fat	4.1g	Sodium	143mg
Saturated Fat	2.3g	Fibre	4.0g
Carbohydrate	8.5g		

Tomato and Onion Bake

Serves 4

2 large tomatoes, sliced

1 large onion, sliced

½ teaspoon dried mixed herbs

pepper to taste

2 tablespoons water

dried chives, to garnish

1 Preheat oven to 180°C. Layer the sliced tomatoes, onion and herbs into a baking dish and then add water.

2 Bake for 30 minutes. Once baked, garnish with dried chives and serve.

chOOz to lOOz **Program**

1 serve = Free

PER SERVE

KJ (cal)	121 (29)	Protein	1.6g
Fat	0.1g	Sodium	11mg
Saturated Fat	0g	Fibre	1.7g
Carbohydrate	4.3g		

Ratatouille

Serves 4

canola or olive oil cooking spray

1 eggplant , sliced

1 medium zucchini, sliced

2 medium onions, thinly sliced

1 red capsicum, sliced

1 Preheat oven to 180°C. Spray a casserole dish with oil and layer the bottom of the casserole dish, first with the eggplant, and then alternating layers of each of the different vegetables.

2 Bake, covered, in an oven for 45 minutes. Uncover and cook for a further 10 minutes.

chOOz to lOOz **Program**

1 serve = Free

PER SERVE

KJ (cal)	164 (39)	Protein	2.1g
Fat	0.3g	Sodium	9mg
Saturated Fat	0g	Fibre	2.7g
Carbohydrate	5.7g		

vegetables & salads

Spiced Chinese Vegetables
Serves 4

canola or olive oil cooking spray
½ teaspoon grated fresh ginger
1 clove garlic, crushed
1 medium onion, cut into wedges
1 cup broccoli florets
½ cup celery, cut into Chinese-style chunks
½ cup zucchini, cut into strips
½ cup carrot, cut into strips
1 cup baby spinach leaves
1 tablespoon soy sauce
1 tablespoon water
1 chicken stock cube

1 Lightly spray a wok with oil, add the ginger, garlic and onions and stir-fry for 2–3 minutes.

2 Add the remaining vegetables and stir-fry for a further 2–3 minutes.

3 Add soy sauce, water and crumbled stock cubes, cover and cook for 2 minutes or until heated through.

S

chOOz to lOOz Program
1–2 serves = Free

PER SERVE			
KJ (cal)	135 (32)	Protein	2.4g
Fat	0.4g	Sodium	553mg
Saturated Fat	0.1g	Fibre	2.3g
Carbohydrate	3.6g		

Italian-Style Celery
Serves 4

canola or olive oil cooking spray
4 cups chopped celery
½ cup grated onion
1 clove garlic, crushed
400g can crushed tomatoes
1 tablespoon basil, chopped

1 Lightly spray a non-stick pan with cooking spray, add the celery, onion, garlic, tomatoes and basil and cook over a medium heat for 3 minutes.

2 Cover and bring to the boil, reduce heat and simmer for 10 minutes.

chOOz to lOOz Program
1–2 serves = Free

PER SERVE			
KJ (cal)	197 (47)	Protein	1.9g
Fat	0.4g	Sodium	176mg
Saturated Fat	0g	Fibre	3.9g
Carbohydrate	7.0g		

Turkish Cucumber Salad

Serves 4

3 medium cucumbers, sliced

1½ cups low-fat plain yoghurt

juice of ½ a lemon

pepper to taste

1 tablespoon mint, chopped

1 tablespoon parsley, chopped

1 tablespoon chives, chopped

paprika, to garnish

1 Put the cucumber into a shallow bowl.

2 Put the yoghurt, lemon juice, herbs and paprika into a bowl and mix to combine.

3 Top the sliced cucumber with the yoghurt dressing.

4 Sprinkle with paprika.

chOOz to lOOz **Program**
1 serve = 1 milk exchange

PER SERVE

KJ (cal)	377 (90)	Protein	5.8g
Fat	1.8g	Sodium	95.5mg
Saturated Fat	1.0g	Fibre	1.0g
Carbohydrate	10.8g		

Tabouli

Serves 8

1½ cups bulghur wheat

1 bunch shallots, sliced

1½ cups parsley, chopped

2 large ripe tomatoes, diced

1 tablespoon mint, chopped

1 medium onion, finely diced

⅓ cup lemon juice

1 tablespoon olive oil

1 Put the bulghur wheat into a bowl, cover with cold water and allow to stand for 30 minutes, drain well.

2 Put the shallots, parsley, tomatoes, mint and onions into a bowl and mix to combine.

3 Whisk together the lemon juice and oil, pour over the salad, and toss well.

chOOz to lOOz **Program**
1 serve = 1 bread exchange
and ½ fat exchange

PER SERVE

KJ (cal)	411 (98)	Protein	2.9g
Fat	3.0g	Sodium	24mg
Saturated Fat	0.4g	Fibre	4.0g
Carbohydrate	12.4g		

vegetables & salads

Asian Beef Salad
Serves 4

500g lean sirloin, rump or fillet steak

1 medium capsicum, sliced

½ cup snow peas

1 cup broccoli florets

250g button mushrooms

Dressing

2 tablespoons soy sauce

1 tablespoon peanut oil

2 tablespoons lemon juice

1 teaspoon crushed garlic

1 teaspoon chopped ginger

1 Cook the steak on a barbecue until done to your liking. Allow to stand for 5 minutes.

2 Steam the snow peas, capsicum strips, broccoli and mushrooms until tender.

3 For the dressing, whisk together the soy sauce, peanut oil, lemon juice, garlic and ginger in bowl.

4 Slice the steaks thinly across the grain, transfer to a bowl, add the vegetables and dressing and toss to combine.

S *chOOz to lOOz* **Program**
1 serve = 3 meat exchanges
and 1 fat exchange

PER SERVE			
KJ (cal)	1017 (243)	Protein	31.6g
Fat	10.6g	Sodium	729mg
Saturated Fat	3.3g	Fibre	2.9g
Carbohydrate	3.3g		

Thai Beef Salad
Serves 4

500g lean sirloin, rump or fillet steak

1 large red onion, sliced

100g bean sprouts

150g button mushrooms, sliced

125g cherry tomatoes

2 medium carrots, julienned

2 Lebanese cucumbers, julienned

Chilli Marinade

1 teaspoon chopped chilli

1 teaspoon crushed garlic

½ cup fresh lemon or lime juice

2 tablespoons *Splenda*

1 teaspoon Thai fish sauce

1 Cook the steaks on a barbecue or in a chargrill pan until done to your liking. Allow to stand for 5 minutes. Thinly slice the steaks across the grain.

2 Put the steak, onion, bean sprouts, mushrooms, tomatoes, carrots and cucumbers into a bowl and mix to combine.

3 For the dressing, whisk together the chilli, garlic, lemon or lime juice, *Splenda* and fish sauce. Pour over the steak and vegetables and toss to combine.

chOOz to lOOz **Program**
1 serve = 3 meat exchanges

PER SERVE

KJ (cal)	966 (231)	Protein	31.0g
Fat	6.1g	Sodium	209mg
Saturated Fat	2.5g	Fibre	4.5g
Carbohydrate	9.5g		

vegetables & salads

Cauliflower, Bean and Carrot Salad
Serves 4

½ cauliflower, cut into small florets

2 cups fresh beans, trimmed and sliced

2 medium carrots, sliced

1 medium onion, sliced into thin rings

¼ cup no-oil French dressing

1 Steam the cauliflower, beans, and carrots for 2 minutes.

2 Remove vegetables from the heat and place directly into some cold water, then drain well and refrigerate until ready to serve.

3 Add the onion and dressing before serving and toss to combine.

PER SERVE			
KJ (cal)	264 (63)	Protein	3.5g
Fat	0.3g	Sodium	197mg
Saturated Fat	0g	Fibre	4.1g
Carbohydrate	9.1g		

Marinated Mushrooms
Serves 4

500g small button mushrooms

½ cup water

⅓ cup white vinegar

1–2 small bay leaves

1 medium white onion, very thinly sliced

1 Place the mushrooms and water into a saucepan and bring to the boil, reduce heat and simmer for 2 minutes, drain the liquid from the mushrooms into another bowl.

2 Place ½ cup of the cooking liquid back into the saucepan and disregard the remaining liquid.

3 Add the vinegar and bay leaves to the mushroom juice in the saucepan and bring to the boil.

4 Place the sliced onion and the cooked mushrooms into a bowl and pour the hot liquid over the mushrooms. Cover and refrigerate overnight.

PER SERVE			
KJ (cal)	194 (46)	Protein	4.9g
Fat	0.4g	Sodium	12.5mg
Saturated Fat	0g	Fibre	3.5g
Carbohydrate	3.2g		

Tangy Broccoli and Corn Salad
Serves 8

2 cups broccoli florets

400g can corn kernels, drained

2 medium zucchini

2 medium tomatoes

1–2 tablespoons balsamic vinegar

pepper, to taste

1 Steam the broccoli until tender. Allow to cool.

2 Put the cooled broccoli, corn, zucchini, tomatoes into a bowl and gently mix to combine.

3 Add the vinegar and pepper to taste, and toss the salad to coat in the dressing.

chOOz to lOOz **Program**
1 serve = Free

PER SERVE			
KJ (cal)	306 (73)	Protein	3.7g
Fat	0.7g	Sodium	144mg
Saturated Fat	0.1g	Fibre	3.8g
Carbohydrate	10.8g		

Italian Mushroom and Zucchini Salad
Serves 4

250g button mushrooms, sliced

juice of 1 lemon

3 zucchini, sliced

2 teaspoons parsley, chopped

1 tablespoon shallots, chopped

1 Put the mushrooms, lemon juice, parsley, zucchini and shallots into a bowl and mix to combine.

2 Cover and refrigerate the mushroom salad for 1 hour before serving.

3 Return the salad to room temperature before serving.

chOOz to lOOz **Program**
1 serve = Free

PER SERVE			
KJ (cal)	144 (34)	Protein	3.3g
Fat	0.4g	Sodium	8mg
Saturated Fat	0g	Fibre	2.8g
Carbohydrate	2.5g		

vegetables & salads

Nutty Green Salad
Serves 4

juice of 2 lemons

Splenda to taste

1 cup bean sprouts

1 cup alfalfa sprouts

1 bunch shallots, chopped

4 sticks celery, thinly sliced

1 cup button mushrooms, sliced

1 tablespoon walnuts, chopped

1 Whisk together the lemon juice and *Splenda* to dissolve.

2 Put the bean sprouts, alfalfa, shallots, celery, mushrooms and walnuts into a bowl and mix to combine.

3 Pour over the dressing and toss to coat.

Vegetables with Creamy Sauce
Serves 2

200g broccoli florets

500g button mushrooms, sliced

500g low-fat plain yoghurt

black pepper to taste

2 tablespoons lemon juice

1 Steam the broccoli and mushrooms until just tender.

2 Gently warm the yoghurt in a saucepan. Do not boil or it will split.

3 Remove from the heat, add the broccoli, mushrooms, pepper and lemon juice and mix to combine. Serve over cooked pasta.

---

chOOz to lOOz Program
1 serve = Free

PER SERVE			
KJ (cal)	190 (46)	Protein	2.6g
Fat	1.8g	Sodium	47mg
Saturated Fat	0.1g	Fibre	2.4g
Carbohydrate	3.0g		

---

chOOz to lOOz Program
1 serve = 1½ milk exchanges

PER SERVE			
KJ (cal)	1019 (244)	Protein	28.6g
Fat	1.6g	Sodium	214mg
Saturated Fat	0.3g	Fibre	10.4g
Carbohydrate	19.8g		

Basic White Sauce

Serves 2

4 tablespoons wholemeal plain flour

4 tablespoons skim milk powder

2 cups cold water

1 Blend the flour, skim milk powder and a little water in a small pan to form a smooth paste.

2 Gradually add the remaining water, stirring constantly until smooth

3 Cook the sauce over a medium heat, stirring constantly until the sauce boils and thickens.

chOOz to lOOz **Program**
1 serve = 1 milk exchange
and ½ bread exchange

PER SERVE

KJ (cal)	553 (132)	Protein	8.6g
Fat	0.6g	Sodium	69mg
Saturated Fat	0.1g	Fibre	2.5g
Carbohydrate	22.0g		

Seafood Sauce

Serves 4

½ cup tomato juice

2 drops Tabasco sauce

½ teaspoon white vinegar

juice of 1 lemon

1 teaspoon Worcestershire sauce

1 teaspoon horseradish

chopped parsley

1 Put the tomato juice, Tabasco sauce, vinegar, lemon juice, Worcestershire sauce, horseradish and parsley into a bowl and mix to combine.

2 Place in the refrigerator and allow to chill until ready to serve.

chOOz to lOOz **Program**
1 serve = Free

PER SERVE

KJ (cal)	117 (28)	Protein	0.8g
Fat	0.3g	Sodium	279mg
Saturated Fat	0.2g	Fibre	0.5g
Carbohydrate	4.4g		

vegetables & salads

Zesty Potato Dressing
Serves 4

1 cup low-fat natural yoghurt

½ teaspoon paprika

¼ cup lemon juice

½ teaspoon mustard

2 teaspoons honey

1 teaspoon grated lemon rind

2 tablespoons chopped chives

1 tablespoons mild curry powder

1 Put the yoghurt, paprika, lemon juice, mustard, honey, lemon rind, chives and curry powder into a bowl and mix to combine.

2 Cover and place the dressing in the refrigerator, allow to chill for 1 hour before serving.

Grainy Italian Dressing
Serves 2

¼ cup water

¼ cup white vinegar

½ teaspoon grain mustard

½ teaspoon paprika

½ teaspoon liquid sweetener

1 tablespoon chopped chives

1 Put the water, vinegar, grain mustard, paprika, sweetener and chives into a jar and shake well to combine.

2 Cover and place the dressing in the refrigerator, allow to chill for 1 hour before serving.

---

chOOz to lOOz **Program**
1 serve = 1 milk exchange

PER SERVE			
KJ (cal)	503 (120)	Protein	8.6g
Fat	1.0g	Sodium	105mg
Saturated Fat	0.2g	Fibre	1.0g
Carbohydrate	16.7g		

---

chOOz to lOOz **Program**
1 serve = Free

PER SERVE			
KJ (cal)	46 (11)	Protein	0.3g
Fat	0.2g	Sodium	12mg
Saturated Fat	0g	Fibre	0.1g
Carbohydrate	0.8g		

Vegie express

- **FLAVOUR BURST** To give cooked vegetables a lift, add a clove of garlic, finely diced onion, fresh herbs, black pepper or onion powder instead of salt.

- **SPEEDY SALAD** Use pre-prepared salad mixes from the supermarket such as coleslaw, Greek, tossed or French. All you do is add a low- or no-oil Italian or French dressing for an instant salad.

- **NOT SO RAW** Cooked vegies such as cauliflower, carrot, beans and broccoli are great in salads. Add orange juice or low-joule dressing and refrigerate.

- **COLOUR YOUR BOWL** Add texture and colour with different combinations of three or more vegetables. Try spinach, lightly cooked green beans, tomato or cherry tomatoes, carrot, cucumber, onion, capsicum, garlic, chives, radish, leeks, grated zucchini, mushrooms, shredded cabbage, parsley, bean sprouts, alfalfa sprouts, rocket, snow peas, snow pea sprouts and cauliflower.

Always rinse salad vegetables thoroughly and pat dry with a tea towel, or use a salad spinner. Serve on chilled plates for the perfect salad experience.

All these recipes contain less than 920KJ (170 calories) per serve.

Moist, light and sweet, these
muffins and cakes are also
healthy! Bake a batch now and
freeze to thaw and enjoy anytime.

muffins
& cakes

muffins & cakes

Oat Bran Fruit and Nut Muffins
Makes 12

2¼ cups oat bran

1 teaspoon baking powder

¼ cup *Splenda*

2 egg whites

1¼ cups skim milk

1 tablespoon canola oil

¼ cup mixed nuts, chopped

¼ cup mixed dried fruit

1 Preheat oven to 200ºC. Lightly grease 12 x ½ cup capacity muffin holes with cooking spray.

2 Put the oat bran, baking powder and *Splenda* into a bowl and mix to combine. Make a well in the centre.

3 Whisk together the egg whites, milk and canola oil. Add to the dry ingredients and mix until just combined.

4 Gently fold through the nuts and dried fruits.

5 Spoon the mixture into the prepare muffin tin and bake for 20 minutes or until the muffins begin to come away from the side of the pan.

---

chOOz to lOOz Program
1 serve = 2 bread exchanges,
or 1 bread and 1 fruit exchange

PER SERVE

KJ (cal)	614 (147)	Protein	6.5g
Fat	4.7g	Sodium	78mg
Saturated Fat	0.7g	Fibre	4.5g
Carbohydrate	17.4g		

Cinnamon Fruit Muffins
Makes 12

1 cup rolled oats

1 cup wholemeal self-raising flour

¼ cup *Splenda*

½ teaspoon ground cinnamon

1 cup skim or low-fat milk

1 egg

¼ cup canola oil

1 large ripe banana

½ cup raisins or sultanas

1 Preheat oven to 200ºC. Lightly grease 12 x ½ cup capacity muffin holes with cooking spray.

2 Put the rolled oats, flour, *Splenda* and cinnamon into a bowl and mix to combine. Make a well in the centre.

3 Whisk together the egg, milk and canola oil. Add to the dry ingredients and mix until just combined.

4 Gently fold through the banana and raisins or sultanas.

5 Spoon the mixture into the prepared muffin tin and bake for 20 minutes or until the muffins begin to come away from the side of the pan.

chOOz to lOOz Program
1 serve = 2 bread exchanges
or 1 bread and 1 fruit exchange

PER SERVE			
KJ (cal)	556 (133)	Protein	3.3g
Fat	5.3g	Sodium	81mg
Saturated Fat	0.6g	Fibre	2.0g
Carbohydrate	17.2g		

muffins & cakes

Banana Bran Muffins
Makes 12

1 cup unprocessed bran

2 cup wholemeal self-raising flour

2 teaspoons baking powder

1 teaspoon cinnamon

1 teaspoon nutmeg

4 eggs

1 cup skim milk

2 teaspoons vanilla essence

6 medium ripe bananas, mashed

1 Preheat oven to 200ºC. Lightly grease 12 x ½ cup capacity muffin holes with cooking spray.

2 Sift the flour, baking powder and spices into a bowl. Add the bran and mix to combine. Make a well in the centre.

3 Whisk together the eggs, milk and vanilla. Gently mix in the mashed banana.

4 Add banana/egg mix to the dry ingredients and fold in until just combined.

5 Spoon the mixture into the prepared muffin tin and bake for 20 minutes or until the muffins begin to come away from the side of the pan.

chOOz to lOOz Program
1 serve = 2 bread exchanges
or 1 bread and 1 fruit exchange

PER SERVE			
KJ (cal)	715 (171)	Protein	7.5g
Fat	2.5g	Sodium	285mg
Saturated Fat	0.6g	Fibre	6.1g
Carbohydrate	26.8g		

Apricot and Carrot Muffins
Makes 12

2 tablespoons canola margarine

1½ cups water

120g dried apricots, diced

120g dried fruit medley

120g wholemeal plain flour

120g wholemeal self-raising flour

½ teaspoon bicarbonate soda

½ teaspoon ground cinnamon

½ teaspoon nutmeg

1 cup grated carrot

1 Preheat oven to 180°C. Lightly grease 12 x ½ cup capacity muffin holes with cooking spray.

2 Place water, margarine and dried fruit in a saucepan. Bring to the boil, then reduce heat, and simmer for 5 minutes. Remove and set aside to cool.

3 Sift the flours, soda and spices into a bowl. Make a well in the centre.

4 Add the grated carrot and cooked fruit mixture and mix until just combined.

5 Spoon the mixture into the prepared muffin tin and bake for 45 minutes or until the muffins begin to come away from the side of the pan.

---

chOOz to lOOz Program
1 serve = 1 bread exchange, plus
1 fruit exchange and 1 fat exchange

PER SERVE

KJ (cal)	717 (171)	Protein	3.9g
Fat	3.9g	Sodium	178mg
Saturated Fat	0.5g	Fibre	5.0g
Carbohydrate	28.0g		

muffins & cakes

Carrot and Date Muffins
Makes 12

240g wholemeal self-raising flour

1 teaspoon ground cinnamon

½ teaspoon bicarbonate soda

½ cup *Splenda*

240g grated carrot

240g grated zucchini

120g pitted dates, chopped

2 eggs

80g canola margarine, melted

125ml skim milk

1 Preheat oven to 180°C. Lightly grease 12 x ½ cup capacity muffin holes with cooking spray.

2 Sift the flour, cinnamon and bicarbonate soda into a bowl. Stir in the *Splenda*, carrot, zucchini and dates. Make a well in the centre.

3 Whisk together the eggs, margarine and milk. Add to the dry ingredients and mix until just combined.

4 Spoon the mixture into the prepared muffin tin and bake for 45 minutes or until the muffins begin to come away from the side of the pan.

chOOz to lOOz Program
1 serve = 1 bread and 1 fruit exchange plus 1 fat exchange

PER SERVE			
KJ (cal)	729 (174)	Protein	4.5g
Fat	6.8g	Sodium	242mg
Saturated Fat	1.1g	Fibre	4.1g
Carbohydrate	22.0g		

Mixed Fruit Cake

Serves 10

440g dried fruit medley, diced

2 cups water

1 large banana, mashed

240g wholemeal self-raising flour

1 teaspoon ground cinnamon

1 teaspoon orange rind

16 walnuts

1 Preheat oven to 180ºC. Lightly grease and line a 20cm cake tin.

2 Put the dried fruit in saucepan with the water. Bring to boil, reduce heat, allow to simmer covered for 5 minutes.

3 Transfer the mixture to a bowl, add the banana, sifted flour, cinnamon and orange rind.

4 Spoon the mixture into the prepared tin and decorate the top with walnuts, bake for 40 minutes or until a skewer comes out clean when inserted into the centre.

5 Allow to cool in tin for 5 minutes before turning out onto a wire rack to cool completely.

chOOz to lOOz Program
1 serve = 1 bread and 1 fruit exchange

PER SERVE

KJ (cal)	686 (164)	Protein	3.5g
Fat	2.0g	Sodium	120mg
Saturated Fat	0.1g	Fibre	4.6g
Carbohydrate	31.3g		

muffins & cakes

Oatmeal and Fruit Loaf
Serves 10

1 cup rolled oats, regular
  or quick-cooking

⅓ cup *Splenda*

1 cup dried fruit

1 cup skim milk

1 cup wholemeal self-raising flour

1 Put the rolled oats, *Splenda* and the dried fruit into a bowl and mix to combine.

2 Heat the skim milk and then pour over the dry ingredients and mix well.

3 Allow to stand while the mixture cools.

4 Preheat oven to 180°C. Grease a 11cm x 21cm loaf tin.

5 Add the self-raising flour to the rolled oats mixture once it is cooled and quickly mix to blend the ingredients, but do not over mix.

6 Pour the loaf mixture into the tin and cook on medium for 40–45 minutes.

7 Leave to cool in tin for 5 minutes before turning out onto a wire rack to cool completely.

chOOz to lOOz Program
1 serve = 1 bread and 1 fruit exchange

PER SERVE			
KJ (cal)	567 (136)	Protein	4.1g
Fat	1.2g	Sodium	108mg
Saturated Fat	0.2g	Fibre	3.4g
Carbohydrate	25.6g		

High Fibre Fruit Loaf
Serves 10

120g *All-Bran*

120g dried apricots, chopped

6 figs, chopped

3 tablespoons *Splenda*

1 teaspoon mixed spice

2½ cups skim milk

160g wholemeal self-raising flour

canola oil cooking spray

1 Preheat oven to 180ºC. Lightly grease 11cm x 21cm loaf tin with cooking spray.

2 Put the *All-Bran*, apricots, figs, *Splenda* and mixed spice into a bowl and mix to combine.

3 Put the milk into a pan and heat until it is just about to boil, pour over the dry ingredients and allow to stand for 5 minutes.

4 Add the sifted flour and husks and mix until just combined.

5 Spoon the mixture into the prepared tin and bake for 40 minutes or until a skewer comes out clean when inserted into the centre.

6 Leave to cool in tin for 5 minutes before turning out onto a wire rack to cool completely.

chOOz to lOOz Program
1 serve = 1 bread and 1 fruit exchange

PER SERVE

KJ (cal)	720 (172)	Protein	6.7g
Fat	1.1g	Sodium	189mg
Saturated Fat	0.2g	Fibre	8.2g
Carbohydrate	30.0g		

muffins & cakes

Fruit Cake
Serves 10

1 cup currants

1 cup raisins

1 cup sultanas

½ cup mixed peel

¼ teaspoon ground cloves

¼ teaspoon nutmeg

1 teaspoon ground cinnamon

1 cup unsweetened pineapple juice

2 cups wholemeal self-raising flour

½ cup skim milk

1 egg, lightly beaten

1 Preheat oven to 180ºC. Lightly grease 14cm x 21cm loaf tin and line the base and sides with baking paper.

2 Put the dried fruit, spices and juice into a large pan and bring to boil, reduce heat, simmer for 3 minutes.

3 Remove from heat, transfer to a bowl and allow to cool.

4 Add the flour, milk and egg and mix to combine.

5 Spoon the mixture into the prepared tin and bake for 45 minutes or until a skewer comes out clean when inserted into the centre.

6 Leave to cool in tin for 5 minutes before turning out onto a wire rack to cool completely.

chOOz to lOOz Program
1 serve = 1 bread and 1 fruit exchange

PER SERVE

KJ (cal)	583 (139)	Protein	3.0g
Fat	0.7g	Sodium	122mg
Saturated Fat	0.2g	Fibre	2.9g
Carbohydrate	29.2g		

Marvellous muffins and cakes

- **SAVE FOR LATER** All these muffins and cakes can be frozen for up to two months, ready to be thawed, reheated and enjoyed at a moment's notice. Just make sure you don't eat them all in one go!

- **WARM IT UP** Muffins warmed up in the microwave are always nice in winter. Top them with reduced-fat cream cheese or ricotta cheese or low-fat yoghurt and 100% fruit jam for variety.

- **FRUITY TREAT** Warm up fruit cake and serve with low-fat and low-sugar varieties of custard, ice cream or yoghurt.

All these recipes contain less than 920KJ (220 calories) per serve.

Nutritious and tasty recipes are essential for happy, healthy kids. Engaging children in the kitchen, garden and supermarket with cooking, growing and shopping will increase their interest in healthy food.

children's recipes

children's recipes

Corn Fritters
Serves 4

2 cups corn kernels

2 eggs, lightly beaten

2 tablespoons plain flour

olive oil spray

1 Put the corn, eggs and flour into a bowl and mix well to combine.

2 Divide the mixture into four and shape into patties.

3 Lightly spray a frypan with olive oil spray and cook the patties over a medium heat until golden brown and heated through.

chOOz to lOOz **Program**
1 serve = 1 ½ bread exchanges
and ½ meat exchange

PER SERVE			
KJ (cal)	606 (145)	Protein	6.4g
Fat	3.5g	Sodium	270mg
Saturated Fat	0.9g	Fibre	2.9g
Carbohydrate	20.4g		

Rice Paper Rolls
Serves 4

100g dried vermicelli noodles, soaked in hot water and drained

½ cup grated carrot

½ cup cabbage, shredded

150g chicken breast fillet, cooked and sliced

mint (optional)

4 sheets rice paper

1 Put the vermicelli, carrot, cabbage, chicken and mint if using, into a bowl and mix well to combine.

2 Soak one sheet of rice paper in lukewarm water until soft. Place onto a clean tea towel on a chopping board. Place 2–3 tablespoons of the filling into the centre.

3 Roll up, folding in the sides to enclose the filling, cover with damp absorbent paper while you prepare the remaining rolls.

chOOz to lOOz **Program**
1 serve = 1 bread exchange
and 1 meat exchange

PER SERVE (WITHOUT DIPPING SAUCE)			
KJ (cal)	621 (148)	Protein	12.2g
Fat	3.2g	Sodium	207mg
Saturated Fat	0.9g	Fibre	0.8g
Carbohydrate	17.2g		

Slim Salmon Loaf
Serves 5

2 cups mashed potato, made
  with skim milk

2 eggs, lightly beaten

1 tablespoon chopped parsley

pepper, to taste

2 x 220gm cans salmon, drained

1 tablespoon grated onion

1 Preheat oven to 180°C. Lightly
  grease 11cm x 21cm loaf tin.

2 Put the potato, egg, parsley, pepper,
  salmon and onion into a bowl and
  mix well to combine.

3 Spoon the mixture into a prepared
  loaf tin or individual baking moulds.

4 Bake for 40 minutes or until set.

chOOz to lOOz Program
1 serve = 2 meat exchanges
and 1 bread exchange

PER SERVE (WITHOUT DIPPING SAUCE)

KJ (cal)	929 (222)	Protein	24.6g
Fat	7.9g	Sodium	551mg
Saturated Fat	2.3g	Fibre	1.8g
Carbohydrate	12.2g		

children's recipes

Vegetable Pikelets
Serves 5

1 small zucchini

1 carrot

1 tablespoon orange juice

½ cup wholemeal self-raising four

½ cup self-raising flour

1 tablespoon brown sugar

1 egg, lightly beaten

¾ cup skim milk

1 teaspoon canola margarine

olive or canola oil cooking spray

1 Grate zucchini and carrot. Place vegetables and orange juice into pan and cook over a medium heat until the vegetables are soft.

2 Sift flour into a bowl, stir in sugar, egg and milk to form a smooth batter.

3 Stir the cooked vegetables into the batter.

4 Heat the margarine in a non-stick frypan, add 1 tablespoon of the batter, cook over a medium heat until bubbles appear and burst on the surface. Before cooking the other side, spray pan with spray oil to prevent second side from sticking. Cook the other side until golden.

---

chOOz to lOOz Program
1 serve = 1½ bread exchanges
and ½ meat exchange

PER SERVE

KJ (cal)	599 (143)	Protein	6.0g
Fat	1.9g	Sodium	228mg
Saturated Fat	0.5g	Fibre	2.6g
Carbohydrate	24.1g		

Healthy Pancakes
Serves 4

1 egg

¾ cup low-fat milk

1 cup wholemeal self-raising flour

canola cooking spray

1 Whisk the egg and milk in a jug. Sift flour into bowl, make a well in the centre.

2 Add the egg mixture to the flour, whisk to form a smooth thick batter, cover and refrigerate for 1 hour.

3 Spray non-stick pan with cooking spray oil, add 1 large tablespoon of mixture to the pan, cook over a medium heat until bubbles appear and burst on the surface. Remember to spray the pan with spray oil again to prevent second side from sticking. Turn over and cook the other side until golden.

> ### chOOz to lOOz Program
> 1 serve = 1½ bread exchanges
> and ½ milk exchange

PER SERVE			
KJ (cal)	669 (160)	Protein	7.7g
Fat	2.7g	Sodium	271mg
Saturated Fat	0.9g	Fibre	3.9g
Carbohydrate	24.2g		

Apricot Bran Loaf
Serves 10

¾ cup dried apricots

¾ cup sultanas

1 cup *All-Bran*

½ cup *Splenda*

1½ cups skim milk

1½ cups wholemeal self-raising flour

1 teaspoon cinnamon

1 Put the apricots, sultanas, *All-Bran* and *Splenda* and milk into a bowl, cover and allow to stand overnight or for minimum 4 hours.

2 Preheat oven to 180°C. Lightly grease a 20 cm x 10cm loaf tin.

3 Sift the flour and cinnamon into a bowl, returning the husks to the bowl. Make a well in the centre. Add the soaked ingredients and mix well to combine.

4 Spoon the mixture into the prepared tin and bake for 45 minutes to 1 hour, or until a skewer comes out clean when inserted into the centre. Allow to cool in tin.

> ### chOOz to lOOz Program
> 1 serve = 1 fruit exchange
> and 1 bread exchange

PER SERVE			
KJ (cal)	600 (143)	Protein	4.6g
Fat	0.7g	Sodium	158mg
Saturated Fat	0.1g	Fibre	4.9g
Carbohydrate	27.3g		

children's recipes

Savoury Muffins
Makes 12

½ cup wholemeal plain flour

½ cup plain flour

2 teaspoons baking powder

2 teaspoons onion powder

4 cooked potatoes, chopped

1 cup steamed and cooled pumpkin, chopped

1 cup steamed broccoli florets, cooled

¼ cup 97% fat-free sun-dried tomatoes, chopped

4 eggs

½ cup skim milk

1 Preheat oven to 190°C. Lightly spray 12 x ½ cup capacity muffin holes with cooking spray to prevent sticking.

2 Sift flours and baking powder into a bowl. Stir in the onion powder. Make a well in the centre.

3 Put the potatoes, pumpkin, broccoli, and tomatoes a bowl. Add to the flour mixture and gently mix to combine.

4 Whisk together the eggs and milk. Add to dry ingredients and mix quickly until just combined, do not over mix or the muffins will be tough.

5 Three-quarters fill greased muffin pans with mixture.

6 Bake for 15 minutes or until muffins spring back when lightly touched. Leave in pan for 5 minutes before turning out on a wire rack to cool.

chOOz to lOOz Program
1 serve = 1 bread exchange and 1 meat exchange

PER SERVE			
KJ (cal)	580 (139)	Protein	7.2g
Fat	2.5g	Sodium	157mg
Saturated Fat	0.7g	Fibre	3.3g
Carbohydrate	19.9g		

Rock Cakes
Makes 12

240g wholemeal self-raising flour

½ teaspoon mixed spice

¼ cup *Splenda*

1 teaspoon grated lemon rind

60g dried apricots or sultanas, chopped

1½ tablespoons canola margarine, melted and cooled

½ cup skim milk

1 egg, lightly beaten

1 Preheat oven to 180°C. Line two baking trays with baking paper.

2 Sift the flour and spice into a bowl, returning the husks to the bowl. Make a well in the centre.

3 Stir in the *Splenda*, lemon rind and dried apricots or sultanas.

4 Whisk together the margarine, milk and eggs and add to the dry ingredients. Mix until just combined.

5 Drop 12 tablespoons of the mixture onto the baking trays, allowing room for the cakes to spread during cooking. Bake for 30 minutes or until the bases are golden brown.

chOOz to lOOz Program
1 serve = 2 bread exchanges (or 1 bread and 1 fruit exchange) and 1 fat exchange

PER SERVE
KJ (cal)	675 (161)	Protein	5.3g
Fat	4.2g	Sodium	230mg
Saturated Fat	0.7g	Fibre	4.0g
Carbohydrate	23.4g		

All these recipes contain less than
1260KJ (300 calories) per serve.

While fresh fruit is the quickest and healthiest dessert choice, there are plenty of other exciting and delicious possibilities.

desserts

desserts

Strawberry Mousse
Serves 4

4 punnets strawberries

8 egg whites

8 tablespoons *Splenda*

1 Put the strawberries into a blender or food processor and blend until smooth.

2 Beat the egg whites and *Splenda* until stiff peaks form.

3 Fold in the strawberry puree. Spoon the mixture into 4 individual serving dishes.

4 Chill before serving.

chOOz to lOOz Program
1 serve = 1 fruit exchange

PER SERVE

KJ (cal)	433 (103)	Protein	11.2g
Fat	0.3g	Sodium	126mg
Saturated Fat	0g	Fibre	5.5g
Carbohydrate	10.7g		

Fantasia Fruit
Serves 4

125g light cream cheese

6 teaspoons sugar-free orange marmalade

1 teaspoon finely grated lemon rind

¼ teaspoon ground cinnamon or ground ginger

200g low-joule vanilla yoghurt

1 medium orange, peeled and sliced

2 small bananas, peeled and sliced

1 medium apple, cored and sliced

1 Put the low-fat cream cheese, marmalade, lemon rind and cinnamon into a bowl and beat using electric beaters until smooth.

2 Stir in the vanilla yoghurt and mix well.

3 Spoon the topping over the fruit and serve, or use as a fruit dip.

chOOz to lOOz Program
1 serve = 1 fruit exchange,
plus 1 milk exchange

PER SERVE

KJ (cal)	688 (165)	Protein	6.9g
Fat	5.4g	Sodium	148mg
Saturated Fat	3.5g	Fibre	2.7g
Carbohydrate	20.9g		

Banana Pie
Serves 6

Crust

2½ cups rolled oats

2 tablespoons apple juice concentrate

2 tablespoons canola oil

Filling

2 ripe bananas

½ cup skim milk powder

2 egg whites

6 dried apricots

2 passionfruit

1 Preheat oven to 200°C. Lightly spray and line the base of a 20cm springform pan.

2 Put the rolled oats into a bowl, add the combined apple juice concentrate and oil and mix well.

3 Press the oat mixture into the pie dish. Bake for 15–20 minutes or until golden brown. Remove and allow to cool.

4 To make the filling, put the bananas, skim milk powder, egg whites and apricots into a blender or food processor and blend until smooth. Stir in the passionfruit.

5 Pour the filling into the cooled pie crust, and refrigerate the pie for 30 minutes before serving.

chOOz to lOOz **Program**
1 serve = 1 fruit exchange,
2 bread exchanges, 1 fat exchange
and ½ a milk exchange

PER SERVE			
KJ (cal)	1234 (295)	Protein	9.4g
Fat	9.6g	Sodium	60mg
Saturated Fat	1.1g	Fibre	4.6g
Carbohydrate	40.6g		

desserts

Light Lemon Cheesecake Mousse
Serves 6

1 packet diet lemon jelly

²/₃ cup boiling water

juice and rind of 2 lemons

250g low-fat cottage cheese

½ cup *Splenda*

375ml can low-fat evaporated milk, refrigerated for 24 hours before use

1 Put the lemon jelly into a bowl, add the boiling water and stir to dissolve the crystals.

2 Add the lemon rind and 1/3 cup of the lemon juice to the jelly mixture. Set aside and allow to cool, but do not allow to set.

3 Meanwhile, put the cottage cheese and *Splenda* into a bowl and beat using electric beaters until smooth and creamy.

4 Put the chilled evaporated milk into a bowl and beat using electric beaters until thick.

5 Fold the cooled jelly and cheese mixture into milk mixture.

6 Pour the mixture into a serving bowl and refrigerate for 24 hours before serving.

chOOz to lOOz Program
1 serve = 1 milk exchange

PER SERVE			
KJ (cal)	449 (107)	Protein	14.3g
Fat	0.7g	Sodium	126mg
Saturated Fat	0.5g	Fibre	0.5g
Carbohydrate	10.2g		

Quick 'n' Easy Cheesecake with Berry Sauce
Serves 10

300g *Uncle Toby's Protein Plus* cereal or *Weight Watchers* muesli

100g canola margarine, melted

150g low-fat ricotta cheese

500g *Yoplait* no-fat banana and honey yoghurt

150g light cream cheese

3 tablespoons *Splenda*

1 packet diet strawberry jelly

½ cup boiling water

200g frozen mixed berries, thawed

1 Lightly grease and line the base of a 20cm springform pan with baking paper.

2 Put the cereal and melted margarine into a bowl and mix to combine. Press into the base of the prepared tin, refrigerate until firm.

3 Put the ricotta, yoghurt, cream cheese and 2 tablespoons *Splenda* into a bowl and beat using electric beaters until smooth.

4 Put the jelly crystals into a bowl, add the boiling water and stir to dissolve. Set aside to cool slightly.

5 Fold the cooled jelly into the yoghurt mixture.

6 Pour into the chilled base and refrigerate for 1 hour or until set.

7 Put the berries and remaining *Splenda* into a pan, and cook over a medium heat to warm the berries. Serve wedges of the cheesecake topped with the berry sauce.

S C

chOOz to lOOz Program
1 serve = 1 bread exchange,
1 milk exchange, ½ fruit exchange
and 2 fat exchanges

PER SERVE			
KJ (cal)	1130 (270)	Protein	11.5g
Fat	12.4g	Sodium	462mg
Saturated Fat	3.9g	Fibre	1.6g
Carbohydrate	26.9g		

desserts

Very Berry Cheesecake
Serves 10

125g *Arnotts Shredded Wheatmeal*, crushed

60g butter, melted

1 tablespoon gelatine

¼ cup hot water

190g light cream cheese

190g extra-light cream cheese

½ cup *Splenda*

375ml can low-fat evaporated milk

1 teaspoon vanilla essence

250g strawberries, halved

1 packet diet raspberry jelly

1 cup hot water

1 Lightly grease and line the base of a 22cm springform pan with baking paper. Put the biscuit crumbs and butter into a bowl and mix to combine.

2 Press into base of the prepared tin and refrigerate until firm.

3 Put the gelatine into a bowl, add the hot water and stir to dissolve, set aside to cool slightly.

4 Put the cream cheese and *Splenda* into a bowl and beat using electric beaters until smooth.

5 Add the evaporated milk, cooled gelatine and vanilla and beat until combined.

6 Pour the mixture over crumb base and refrigerate for 1 hour or until set.

7 Dissolve the jelly crystals in hot water and allow to cool, but not to set.

8 Arrange the sliced strawberries over the top of set cheesecake, slowly pour over cooled jelly. Refrigerate until set.

C

chOOz to lOOz Program
1 serve = 1 milk exchange,
½ bread exchange, ½ fruit exchange
and 1 fat exchange

PER SERVE			
KJ (cal)	852 (204)	Protein	9.2g
Fat	11.3g	Sodium	255mg
Saturated Fat	7.1g	Fibre	1.3g
Carbohydrate	16.2g		

Fromage Blanc

Serves 2

125g low-fat vanilla, 'no added sugar' yoghurt

100g low-fat cottage cheese

3 teaspoons lemon juice

1 Put the vanilla yoghurt, cottage cheese and lemon juice into a food processor and blend until smooth and creamy.

2 Divide the mixture between two serving glasses and refrigerate until set.

PER SERVE			
KJ (cal)	330 (79)	Protein	12.5g
Fat	0.7g	Sodium	111mg
Saturated Fat	0.5g	Fibre	0g
Carbohydrate	4.8g		

Banana Fool

Serves 2

100g low-fat cottage cheese

125g low-fat vanilla yoghurt, no added sugar

2 medium ripe bananas, mashed

2 tablespoons *Splenda*

1 Put the cottage cheese, yoghurt, banana and *Splenda* into a food processor and blend until smooth and creamy.

2 Divide the mixture between two serving dishes and refrigerate until chilled.

PER SERVE			
KJ (cal)	730 (175)	Protein	14.1g
Fat	0.8g	Sodium	113mg
Saturated Fat	0.5g	Fibre	2.2g
Carbohydrate	26.3g		

desserts

Apple and Sultana Strudel
Serves 4

4 medium apples, peeled, cored and sliced

60g sultanas

ground cinnamon, to taste

1–2 tablespoons lemon juice

2 slices Mountain bread

1 Preheat oven to 200°C. Put the apples, sultanas, cinnamon and lemon juice into a bowl and mix to combine.

2 Spoon the apple mixture down the centre of each slice of bread and roll up the bread, folding in the sides to enclose the filling.

3 Place seam side down onto a non-stick baking tray. Bake for 20 minutes or until the apples are cooked when tested with a skewer.

chOOz to lOOz Program
1 serve = 1 bread exchange,
plus 1½ fruit exchanges

PER SERVE			
KJ (cal)	701 (168)	Protein	2.3g
Fat	0.4g	Sodium	142mg
Saturated Fat	0.1g	Fibre	4.3g
Carbohydrate	37.6g		

Banana Pancakes
Serves 4

80g plain flour

80g wholemeal plain flour

1 teaspoon baking powder

2 eggs, lightly beaten

2 cups skim milk

2 medium ripe bananas, mashed

canola cooking spray

1 Sift the flours and baking powder into a bowl. Make a well in centre.

2 Whisk together the eggs, skim milk and banana. Add to the dry ingredients and mix to form a smooth batter.

3 Spray a non-stick fry pan with cooking spray. Add ¼ of the mixture into the pan, cook over a medium heat until bubbles burst at the surface. Remember to spray pan again with cooking spray before turning the pancake over and cooking the other side until golden. Repeat with the remaining mixture.

chOOz to lOOz Program
1 serve = 2 bread exchanges,
½ fruit exchange and ½ milk exchange

PER SERVE			
KJ (cal)	1116 (267)	Protein	13.4g
Fat	3.4g	Sodium	240mg
Saturated Fat	1.0g	Fibre	4.1g
Carbohydrate	43.8g		

Orange Cottage and Custard Cake

Serves 6

Base

2½ cups *Bran Flakes*, crushed

2 tablespoons canola margarine, melted

pinch of ground cinnamon

1 tablespoon *Splenda*

2 tablespoons plain flour

Filling

240g cottage cheese

4 eggs, lightly beaten

1 teaspoon plain flour

2 teaspoons *Splenda*

½ teaspoon grated orange or lemon rind

600g oranges, peeled and segmented

canola cooking spray

1 Preheat oven to 180°C. Lightly spray the base of a 20cm springform pan with cooking spray.

2 To make the base, put the *Bran Flakes*, margarine, cinnamon, *Splenda* and plain flour into a bowl and mix to combine. Press the mixture into the base of the prepared tin. Bake for 5 minutes or until golden brown.

3 Put the cottage cheese, eggs, flour, *Splenda*, and orange or lemon rind in a bowl and beat using electric beaters until smooth and creamy.

4 Arrange the segmented orange slices over the cooled crumb base. Pour the cheese mixture over the fruit.

5 Bake for 40–45 minutes or until the mixture is set and golden brown.

S

chOOz to lOOz Program
1 serve = 1 bread and 1 fruit exchange, ½ milk exchange and 1 fat exchange

PER SERVE			
KJ (cal)	1002 (259)	Protein	13.5g
Fat	11.5g	Sodium	344mg
Saturated Fat	3.4g	Fibre	4.9g
Carbohydrate	22.8g		

3

Healthy Plan

time for change

Permanent weight loss is a challenge. We all know that to lower our weight we need to consume fewer kilojoules and burn up more through increased activity. Make a choice to start today.

> Eat only when you are hungry – food tastes better, and it's easier to know when to stop.

PERMANENT WEIGHT LOSS starts with some clear choices: you need to eat more nutritious, low-kilojoule foods, limit low-nutrient, high-kilojoule foods and you must ramp up your activity levels. I can't swim laps for you or take your place in a step class, but I can get you started on the right path. Part 3, *Healthy Start* contains two weekly menu plans using recipes from Part 2. It's based on the successful *chOOz to lOOz* program and follows the *Dietary guidelines for Australians*. Each weekly menu has its own shopping list – it's a foolproof way to ensure that you have all the ingredients at hand to begin your program. Then, make sure your mind is in the right place – set some realistic goals and go for them.

SIMPLE GUIDELINES FOR WEIGHT LOSS

■ Eat three regular, balanced meals a day and up to three healthy snacks a day when hungry.

■ Include foods from each food group in the right amounts. Follow the *Dietary guidelines for Australians* on page 17. Refer to the Exchange list on page 171 for healthy dietary variations.

■ Be as active as you can. Get regular exercise that you enjoy and vary your activites to keep it interesting. Burn more energy in everyday activities – you'll easily increase your overall energy expenditure.

■ Always consult your doctor before starting a weight-loss program. If you need specific dietary advice, log on to **www.daa.asn.au** to find an accredited practising dietitian in your area.

Planning for success

- **GET REAL** Set realistic goals – your weight-loss efforts won't last if you're unhappy or too rigid.

- **JUST REWARDS** Reward yourself when you achieve a goal, no matter how small. For example, if you manage to slow down your eating or if you lose a kilo, buy yourself a favourite magazine or plan a special outing to celebrate.

- **MIND MOTIVATION** Understand what motivates you to lose weight. Make a list and review it often.

- **TEMPT ME NOT** Throw out or give away foods you shouldn't consume often (think: biscuits, cakes, chips), particularly if you can't stop once you start.

- **EMOTIONAL RESCUE** Learn to recognise your emotional triggers and head them off at the pass. If watching TV bores you, and seeing a food advert starts you salivating, then change the channel, pick up a book, or go for a walk around the block.

- **SIMPLY STUNNING** Buy a gorgeous outfit a size smaller than your current size as an incentive to lose weight. Put it in a place where you'll see it daily.

Good taste, good sense

It's important to feel positive, not deprived, when following the menu plans. Dieting doesn't mean you should stop enjoying food. The recipes in Part 2, *Healthy Cook* include plenty of tasty treats, and the weight-loss plans in this section allow for small weekly indulgences. Choose your favourites from the weekly 'extras' column in the Exchange List and enjoy them! Eat them slowly and leave the guilt behind.

You should accept the occasional overindulgence too. Try to learn from these experiences but don't wallow in self-pity. Understand your triggers so that you can reduce the risk next time.

Train yourself to taste food better. Use the hundreds of tastebuds on your tongue to savour every mouthful. Chew food slowly and keep it in your mouth for as long as possible. Also, it takes about 20 minutes for the stomach to register to the brain that it's full, so slow down. Otherwise, you could overeat.

Move it
Burn those kilojoules!
- Try a variety of exercise options. Ride a bike, go to the gym, take a brisk walk, try yoga.
- Discover a new activity that burns energy. Take a friend along!
- Leave the lift and take the stairs.
- Do some housework – vacuum floors or clean windows while listening to a CD.

action plan

The menu plans and shopping lists that follow are useful if you prefer a structured weight-loss program. You'll also learn how to combine recipes to create your own healthy eating plans.

THE TWO-WEEK menu plan averages 6,270 kilojoules (1,500 calories) per day, which is suitable for most adults needing to lose weight. Each day in the weekly menu plan is nutritionally balanced, so if one or two days do not suit you, repeat one or two of the preferred day's menu.

If you are overweight, the menu plan can, in most cases, help you lose around half a kilogram per week. It also ensures you get the right balance of nutrients from the recommended food groups and helps you cut your fat, sugar and salt intake. You can still follow the program to ensure a balanced diet even if you're not trying to lose weight. Just make sure you eat larger portions, enjoy more snacks and have a few more indulgences a week.

Kilojoule needs?

Personal kilojoule needs are based on factors such as gender, age, height, how much activity you do each day, basal metabolism and body type. The energy requirement for weight maintenance in adult women ranges from 7,100 to 10,500kj per day. For men, it's 7,400 to 13,800 kj per day.

Varying menu plans

Use the Exchange list (page 171) to vary options within food groups. For example, if you don't want three *Weet-Bix* for breakfast on Day 2, Week 1, have one cup of *Fibre Plus* or half a cup of raw oats or two slices of bread; each equals two exchanges of cereal or bread.

Feel free to share the recipes and be guided by the plans when it comes to feeding the whole family, although the program is not intended as a weight-reducing eating plan for children. Active and hungry children or teenagers may need larger serves at meals and extra snacks.

Be patient: positive dietary and exercise changes take from three weeks to three months to become new habits.

Menu plan checklist

This guide makes sure you purchase the correct product types so you get the most out of the menu plans.

○ MILK including flavoured is 1% fat or less

○ CHEESE is reduced-fat (around 25% fat)

○ OIL is olive or canola oil. MARGARINE is canola margarine

○ CREAM CHEESE is light

○ YOGHURT is low-fat and, if flavoured, has no added sugar

○ ICE CREAM is at least 97% fat-free

○ MEAT AND CHICKEN should be lean and have no fat or skin

○ WINE glasses are 120ml or ½ cup

○ SALAD DRESSINGS and mayonnaise are low kilojoule, no or low oil

○ WEIGHTS of meat, chicken and fish when indicated are cooked:
  • 90g cooked meat = 120g raw weight
  • 135g cooked chicken = 180g raw weight
  • 180g cooked fish = 250g raw weight
  Use raw weight if measuring before you cook

○ CANNED FISH is drained weight. Tuna is in springwater; salmon is in brine

○ BREADS, muffins, crumpets, and crackers and crispbreads are wholemeal or wholegrain

○ FRUIT, if tinned or packaged, is unsweetened and drained. Berries can be fresh or frozen

○ MIXED SALAD is lettuce, tomato, cucumber, alfalfa sprouts and carrot. Add to this list from the Free vegetables list (p. 174)

○ CHOCOLATE allowance is 30g = e.g. 1 *Flake* or 2 *Freddos*

make it personal

The weekly menu plans are based on the Exchange list. Use this list to vary meals to suit your own preferences. Strive to include the same number of exchanges from each group for each day and one extra each week.

Too much, too little?

If you lose more than 1 kilogram per week, find you get very hungry, or if you are a very active woman or moderately active man, increase your intake by adding up to three exchanges or serves per day.

If you don't lose weight at this level or find that it is too much food to eat, reduce your intake by taking away up to two exchanges from the meat and bread or starchy vegetable exchanges. If you take away two exchanges, take one away from each food group.

THE EXCHANGE LIST places foods of similar nutrient value into different food groups. Nutritional balance requires you have a minimum number of exchanges or serves from each of the food groups for each day and each week. If you devise your own menus, aim to have three regular meals per day, as well as one to three snacks.

For further nutrient intake and variety, vary the exchanges within each food group – if you don't like pasta, swap it for rice (both are grains and in the bread group). If broccoli is out of season, have another vegetable, such as spinach. Refer to your Free lists (pages 172–174) for additional foods and include at least 2½ cups of Free vegetables each day.

Fair trade

You can trade between the bread, fruit and meat groups on the Exchange list. On days when seven exchanges of bread or starchy vegetable is chosen, choose five serves of meat or meat substitute; if you choose six serves of bread, choose six serves of meat or meat substitute.

People with higher energy needs should choose an extra two serves of bread, cereal or starchy vegetable and an extra serve of meat or meat substitute each day.

Healthy swap

Switch your snacks around based on your hunger level over the day. You can always save your snack for later if you're not hungry at that time. Be flexible.

You can also swap the order of your meals and snacks on any one day. There's nothing to stop you having breakfast for dinner or vice versa, if you prefer. You can also combine two snacks together and make a larger snack or include your snacks at meals, if you wish. The key is to keep it interesting.

exchange list

DAILY					WEEKLY
TRADE					
Bread, cereals and starchy vegetables	Fruit	Meat and meat substitute	Milk and dairy products	Fats	Weekly 'extras'
6–7 exchanges	2 exchanges	5–6 exchanges	3 exchanges	2 exchanges	1 exchange
1 exchange =	1 exchange =	1 exchange =	1 exchange =	1 exchange =	1 exchange =
1 slice bread (30g)	1 average fruit e.g. apple, banana, orange*	30g (1 slice) lean lamb, pork or beef	1 cup low-fat, high-calcium milk*	1 tsp of butter/ margarine*	A high-fat main meal
½ bread roll or muffin	2 slices pineapple*	45g (2 slices) poultry (no skin), or veal	200g low-fat, no-sugar yoghurt*	2 tsp cream or salad dressing	60g chocolate
1 crumpet	2–3 smaller fruits, e.g. plum, apricot	60g (2 tbsp) fish or seafood	150g *Fruche Lite*	1 tsp of oil* or mayonnaise	80g lollies
¼ packet rice crackers	½ medium rockmelon	1 egg	40g (2 slices) reduced-fat cheese	1 tbsp avocado*	50g crisps
2 *Ryvita, Sao, Vitawheat*	1 cup grapes, cherries, berries*	130g baked beans, cooked legumes	100g cottage or ricotta cheese	1 tbsp light sour cream	6 plain biscuits, e.g. *Yoyo*
1 *Man-size Salada*	30g dried fruit (1 heaped tbsp)	15g nuts or seeds	2 tbsp light cream cheese		3 fancy biscuits, e.g. chocolate or cream
½ cup *All-Bran Sultana Bran, Plus Fibre Mix*	½ cup juice, unsweetened	20g or 1 slice full-fat cheese	2 scoops low-fat ice cream		2 muesli bars
¾ cup *Bran Flakes*	½ cup tinned or stewed fruit, unsweetened	30g or 1½ slices reduced-fat cheese	½ cup low-fat custard with no added sugar		1 slice of cake
¼ cup rolled oats or muesli		70g or 2 tbsp cottage or ricotta cheese			1 bun
1½ *Weet-Bix, Vitabrits*		1½ tbsp light cream cheese			4 glasses of wine (120ml)
⅓ cup cooked rice					2 stubbies of beer
½ cup cooked pasta					3 stubbies of light beer
1 egg-size potato		*All weights are for cooked foods*		¤Use level tsp	4 measures of spirits
1 scoop mashed potato		*30y –*			
1½ cups popcorn		*1 average slice*			
	*High in vitamin C	Choose at least 4 non-dairy exchanges per day	*Choose these exchanges mostly to ensure adequate calcium	*Choose these fat exchanges more often for essential fats. Choose olive or canola-based oils or margarines.	

boredom beaters

You can eat more than just the foods listed in the Exchange list. The items listed here, all of which should be found in a well-stocked pantry, can be used freely to improve flavour and variety.

Free seasonings, condiments and sweeteners

- herbs
- parsley
- salt*
- artificially sweetened pickles
- caraway/dill/poppy seeds (2 tsp)
- pickled onions/gherkins (4–6)
- salsa
- spices
- mint
- baking soda
- pepper
- lemon/lime juice
- tomato paste/purée*
- tomato sauce (2 tsp)
- chutney or pickles (2 tsp)
- garlic
- curry powder
- mustard*
- vinegar
- stock cubes*
- relish (2 tsp)
- horseradish
- capers
- artificial sweetener – liquid, tablet, powder

Free spreads

- yeast extracts*
- meat and fish pastes* (2 tsp)
- low-joule jam/marmalade
- vegetable spreads
- 100% fruit spreads, no added sugar

* These foods are high in salt, so use sparingly. Excessive salt intake may be associated with high blood pressure. Choose low- or no-salt alternatives where possible. Refer to the *AHSG* for specific brand names. For weight control, the recommended maximum daily limit for foods or fluids is indicated in brackets.

Free beverages

- water
- plain, unflavoured mineral water
- flavoured, unsweetened mineral water
- soda water
- diet soda stream
- diet soft drinks
- diet cordials
- diet energy drinks
- tea, coffee (black, or with milk from allowances)
- non-medicinal herbal teas
- carob/cocoa powder/ *Milo* or *Nestle Caro/ Ecco* powder (2 tsp) or low-joule chocolate drinks (1 sachet only)
- chicory essence
- *Angostura Bitters*
- *Bonox* or *Bovril**
- soup cubes
- clear soup
- fat-free broths
- low-joule packet soups or low-joule canned soups (1 serve only)
- tomato/vegetable juice (½ cup)

Free sauces and dressings

- soy sauce*
- hoisin sauce*
- barbecue sauce*
- chilli sauce*
- Tabasco sauce
- Worcestershire sauce*
- fish sauce/oyster sauce*
- mint sauce
- low-joule, low-oil or no-oil salad dressings
- finishing sauces
- low-joule gravy
- non-stick sprays

Free desserts and sweets

- low-joule jellies
- junket tablets
- gelatine
- flavour essence (vanilla, almond)
- low-joule ice cream toppings
- chewing gum, no added sugar
- sugar-free lollies
- rhubarb (1 cup cooked)
- passionfruit (2)
- lemon (2)

free food

Crisp salads and fresh vegies add nutrients, flavour and bulk to meals, making you feel satisfied for longer. You can eat these foods to your heart's content – they're completely guilt-free.

Free vegetables and salads - have at least 2½ cups per day

- alfalfa sprouts
- artichokes
- asparagus
- bamboo shoots
- beans, green
- beansprouts
- beetroot (4 slices)
- broadbeans (½ cup)
- broccoli
- carrots (1 cup)
- cabbage
- capsicum
- cauliflower
- celery
- chives
- choko
- corn (½ cob or ¼ cup)

- cucumber
- eggplant
- endive
- English spinach
- fennel
- garlic
- kale
- leeks
- lettuce
- marrow
- mushrooms
- mustard and cress
- okra
- onions
- parsley
- parsnips (½ cup)
- peas (½ cup)

- pumpkin (1 cup)
- radishes
- sauerkraut
- shallots
- silverbeet
- snowpeas
- spring onions
- sprouts
- squash
- swedes
- tomatoes
- Turnips
- water chestnuts
- watercress
- witloff
- zucchini

For weight control, the recommended maximum daily limit for foods is indicated in brackets.

Mix and match

Be creative and devise your own menus based on the weekly plans. Remember these essential points:

1 Aim to have at least *THREE REGULAR MEALS* a day and one to three snacks.

2 Aim to include nutrient-rich *WHOLEGRAIN BREAKFAST CEREALS* at least three times a week.

3 Include *RED MEAT* three to four times a week and *FISH* twice a week at your main meals.

4 Have at least two serves of FRUIT a day, five serves of MEAT/ MEAT SUBSTITUTE and five serves of BREAD or starchy vegetable or cereal a day.

5 If you are *VEGETARIAN* and do not include meat, chicken or fish in your menus, consult an accredited practising dietitian to balance your diet.

6 *SWAP* between food groups. Have an extra fruit or meat serve if you have one less bread serve. You can trade between meat, bread and fruit.

7 To reduce the *GLYCAEMIC INDEX* (GI) of a meal and feel fuller for longer, combine your carbohydrates (fruit, bread, cereals and starchy vegetables) with protein (meat/meat substitute) or dairy foods at each main meal.

8 If you require *MORE KILOJOULES*, increase to an extra three exchanges a day (see page 170).

week 1 plan

DAY 1	DAY 2	DAY 3	DAY 4
Breakfast 1 muffin with 1 tbsp light cream cheese and tomato	**Breakfast** 3 *Weet-Bix* with ½ cup milk 100g yoghurt	**Breakfast** 375ml *Feel Good* milk 1 serve fruit (e.g. pear)	**Breakfast** 1 cup *Sultana Bran* with ¾ cup milk
Morning snack Skim milk cappuccino	**Morning snack** 1 banana	**Morning snack** 1 slice raisin toast with 1 tbsp light cream cheese 1 *Jarrah Choc-o-lait*	**Morning snack** 250ml flavoured milk
Lunch 1 roll with slice avocado, 60g tuna, 1 cup mixed salad, low fat dressing 1 apple	**Lunch** 1 cup Creamy of Celery and Onion Soup p.62 Pita pocket with 45g turkey and 1 cup salad	**Lunch** Sandwich with 1 slice avocado, 30g ham and 1½ cups mixed salad	**Lunch** 1 slice thick bread with 1 tbsp tomato paste, asparagus, 30g reduced-fat cheese and ¼ avocado 140g fruit snack pack
Afternoon snack 3 *Vitawheat* with sliced tomato and carrot and celery sticks	**Afternoon snack** Carrot and Date Muffin (p.140) 1 *Jarrah Choc-o-lait*	**Afternoon snack** 1 slice Fruit Cake (p.144) 150g *Fruche Lite*	**Afternoon snack** Large *Salada* with 1 tbsp cream cheese, cucumber and tomato
Dinner Coriander Yoghurt Chicken p.98 with ⅔ cup cooked brown rice and 1 cup steamed broccoli	**Dinner** 90g grilled steak, 1 medium jacket potato with 1 tbsp light sour cream and Ratatouille (p.123), and 1½ cups mixed salad with Grainy Italian Dressing (p.132)	**Dinner** Hearty Minestrone (p.67) Salmon Dip with Vegetable Sticks (p.48)	**Dinner** Fish Provençal (p.74) with 1 cup cooked pasta and 1 cup steamed broccoli
Bedtime snack ½ cup tinned apricots with 2 scoops low-fat ice cream	**Bedtime snack** 200g diet yoghurt with 200g berries	**Bedtime snack** 1 serve Strawberry Mousse (p.156)	**Bedtime snack** 30g dried fruit (e.g. 1 tbsp sultanas) with 15g almonds
Extras 1 cup milk	**Extras** 1 cup milk	**Extras** 1 cup milk	**Extras** 1 cup milk

DAY 5	DAY 6	DAY 7
Breakfast 2 crumpets with 3 tsp peanut paste and 1 tsp margarine	**Breakfast** Banana Pancakes (p.162) with 100g vanilla yoghurt	**Breakfast** 2 slices toast with 1 scrambled egg, 1 diced tomato and ½ cup sliced mushrooms
Morning snack 200g yoghurt 1 orange	**Morning snack** 15g peanuts 1 fruit snack pack	**Morning snack** 1 *Jarrah Choc-o-lait*
Lunch Vegetable Minestrone (p.59) 2 slices bread with 45g chicken with lettuce, tomato, cucumber, onion and mayo	**Lunch** 1 cup Creamy Celery and Onion Soup (p.62) Toasted sandwich with tomato and 30g reduced-fat cheese	**Lunch** Roast Vegetable Pasta (p.119)
Afternoon snack 1 slice High Fibre Fruit Loaf (p.143)	**Afternoon snack** Fruit smoothie – 200g yoghurt, 100ml water and 100g berries	**Afternoon snack** ½ punnet strawberries with 30g melted chocolate dipper e.g. 1 *Flake* or 2 *Freddos*
Dinner Easy Beef Casserole (p.88) with garlic mash (200g mashed potato)	**Dinner (restaurant))** Warm Chicken Salad with dressing and 2 small rolls 2 glasses of wine	**Dinner** Beef in Red Wine Sauce (p.83) with ⅔ cup brown basmati rice
Bedtime snack 1 *Jarrah Choc-o-lait* 1 pear	**Bedtime snack** 1½ cups air-popped popcorn	**Bedtime snack** Apple and Sultana Strudel (p.162) and ½ cup no-sugar custard
Extras ¾ cup milk	**Extras** ¾ cup milk	**Extras** ¾ cup milk

Menu plan breakdown (average per day)

101g protein	(26%)
35g fat	(20%)
2g saturated fat	(6%)
182g carbohydrate	(47%)
3.5g alcohol	(1%)
32.5g fibre	

week 1 shopping

Fruit and vegetables

tomatoes

cherry tomatoes

avocado

carrots

mushrooms

champignon mushrooms (500g)

variety of salad vegetables

variety of vegetables for steaming

celery

onions

potatoes

Japanese pumpkin

leek

green beans

broccoli

shallots

parsley

turnip

sweet potato

chives

cabbage

capsicum

eggplant

baby spinach

zucchini

garlic

lemon

Fruit and vegetables (cont.)

fresh or frozen berries

punnets of strawberries (5)

variety of fresh fruit (10+)

apples (4)

bananas (2)

Dairy and refrigerated items

skim milk

Fruche (2 x 150g)

Philadelphia light cream cheese

tubs of diet yoghurt (200g)

Feel Good flavoured milk (1litre)

small block of reduced-fat cheese

reduced-fat ricotta cheese

low-fat fetta cheese

shaved parmesan

light sour cream

low-fat plain yoghurt (500g)

low-fat ice cream

Canola margarine

frozen peas

Breads, cereals, and pantry items

bread, wholegrain or rye

loaf of raisin bread

wholemeal pita bread (small)

wholegrain rolls

wholemeal English muffins

wholemeal crumpets

Mountain bread

Sanitarium Weet-Bix

Kellogg's Sultana Bran

wholemeal flour

wholemeal self-raising flour

plain white flour

Jarrah Choc-o-lait

small can of salmon in brine

small can tuna in springwater

fat-free salad dressing

low-fat mayonnaise

wholemeal pasta

pasta sauce

basil pesto

tomato paste

brown rice

crackers – *Vitawheat, Salada*

air-popped popcorn

beef stock liquid

stock cubes

coriander

cumin

turmeric

Breads, cereals, and pantry items (cont.)	Breads, cereals, and pantry items (cont.)	Meats, poultry, seafood and eggs
thyme	dried dates	skinless chicken breasts (4)
paprika	mixed nuts	sliced meat from deli section
mixed herbs	Custard powder	– lean turkey, chicken, ham
bay leaves	*Weight Watchers* fruit snack packs	steak
peppercorns	peanut paste	2.7kg lean beef chuck steak
basil	unsweetened pineapple juice	*Note: 1.5 kg of this makes 3 basic beef bases for 3 casserole recipes. You can freeze remaining 2 serves. The extra 1.2 kg is for the Easy Beef Casserole recipe*
bi-carb soda	unsweetened tomato juice	
baking powder	canned tomatoes	
grain mustard	canned asparagus	
canola oil	kidney beans	
pepper	chocolate bar (30g)	eggs
brown sugar		lean bacon
Splenda powder		beef bones
liquid sweetener		boneless fish fillets, e.g. whiting
cinnamon		
ground cloves		
nutmeg		
lemon juice		
balsamic vinegar		
white vinegar		
red wine		
white wine		
canned fruit in natural juice		
dried fruit		
currants		
raisins		
sultanas		
mixed peel		
dried apricots		

SHOPPING LIST TIP

■ The weekly shopping lists are compiled using the week's menu. They don't take into account what you may have purchased the previous week. Always check what you have left over. You may have some of the items required already.

week 2 plan

DAY 1	DAY 2	DAY 3	DAY 4
Breakfast 2 slices rye bread with 3 tbsp cottage cheese, sliced tomato and cracked pepper	**Breakfast** 1 slice of toast with scrape of *Vegemite*, 1 egg and 2 kiwi fruit	**Breakfast** ½ cup natural muesli with ¾ cup milk and ½ cup canned apricots	**Breakfast** 1 cup *Sultana Bran* with ½ cup milk 100g yoghurt
Morning snack	**Morning snack** 1½ cups air-popped popcorn	**Morning snack** 1 apple	**Morning snack** 30g unsalted nuts/seed mix
Lunch 50g Mountain bread wrap with 45g chicken breast, 20g or 1 slice avocado and 1½ cups mixed salad	**Lunch** 2 slices bread with 30g roast beef, 1½ cups mixed salad and low-joule, oil-free dressing	**Lunch** ½ cup couscous with 120g low-fat flavoured tuna and 1½ cups mixed salad 1 apple	**Lunch** Sweet Potato and Leek Soup (p.65) Impossible Mediterranean Pie (p.93)
Afternoon snack 1 cup strawberries 250ml *Feel Good* flavoured milk	**Afternoon snack** 2 *Vitawheat* with 30g cheese	**Afternoon snack** Carrot and Date Muffin (p.139)	**Afternoon snack** 1 apple and celery sticks
Dinner Stuffed Red Capsicums (p.86) with ⅔ cup brown basmati rice and 1 cup steamed broccoli	**Dinner** Pumpkin and Cauliflower Soup (p.57) 180g fish with ½ cup each steamed green beans and carrots and ½ cup couscous	**Dinner** Vegetable Minestrone (p.59), Gourmet Tuna Rice Pie (p.76) with 1½ cups mixed salad topped with 15g shaved parmesan cheese and low-joule, oil-free dressing	**Dinner** 1 cup cooked pasta with Easy Tomato and Vegetable Pasta Sauce (p.118) topped with 25g grated reduced-fat cheese
Bedtime snack 15g unsalted peanuts	**Bedtime snack** ½ cup custard with ½ cup canned peaches set in diet jelly	**Bedtime snack** 1 sliced banana with 1 scoop of ice cream, 15g crushed nuts and diet chocolate topping	**Bedtime snack** 30g chocolate bar
Extras 1 cup milk	**Extras** 1 cup milk	**Extras** 1 cup milk	**Extras** 1 cup milk

DAY 5	DAY 6	DAY 7
Breakfast ½ cups oats with 30g dried fruits and 1 cup milk	Breakfast 30g bacon with 1 poached egg, cooked tomato and mushrooms, 1 slice of toast and ½ cup blackcurrant juice	Breakfast ½ cup *Plus Fibre Mix* plus ½ cup *All-Bran*, with 1 cup milk and ½ sliced banana
Morning snack Pumpkin and Cauliflower Soup (p.57)	Morning snack	Morning snack
Lunch 1 cup pasta with Easy Tomato and Vegetable Pasta Sauce (leftover) with 25g cheese 2 slices pineapple	Lunch (at coffee shop) ½ baguette with 45g turkey, ½ cup salad leaves, cranberry sauce and 15g brie cheese 1 skim milk cappuccino	Lunch Cheesey Spinach and Corn Pie (p.116) 1½ cups mixed salad with low-joule dressing
Afternoon snack 3 *Corn Thins* with 1 tbsp hummus, carrot and celery sticks	Afternoon snack ¼ packet rice crackers (10), 2 tbsp Tzatziki Dip (p.46), salsa, carrot and celery sticks 2 glasses of wine	Afternoon snack 5 almonds, 1 serve of fruit, e.g. 2 slices of pineapple
Dinner Pumpkin and Lentil Curry (p.111) with ½ cup cooked basmati rice and Turkish Cucumber Salad (p.125)	Dinner (or dinner party) Quick Cream of Asparagus Soup (p.59) 90g marinated steak, barbecued, with ½ cup garlic-flavoured sweet potato mash and Tangy Broccoli and Corn Salad (p.129)	Dinner 90g roast beef with 2 egg-size foil-baked potatoes, 1 cup baked pumpkin cubes, ½ cup steamed green vegetables and ½ cup peas
Bedtime snack 1 serve fruit e.g. ¼ large rockmelon	Bedtime snack Fantasia Fruit (p.156)	Bedtime snack Quick'n'Easy Cheesecake with Berry Sauce (p.159)
Extras ¾ cup milk	Extras ¾ cup milk	Extras 1 cup milk

Diabetics:
Your dietitian
may advise you
to include more
or fewer snacks.
If you are insulin-
dependent, you
will probably
need three
regular, carefully
balanced snacks
a day, spaced
evenly between
your meals.

week 2 shopping

Fruit and vegetables

tomatoes

sundried tomatoes, 97% fat free

avocado

capsicums

garlic

onions (white and brown)

mushrooms

green beans

baby spinach

brussel sprouts

peas

carrots

zucchini

pumpkin

cabbage

celery

turnip

parsley

chives

broccoli

cauliflower

sweet potatoes

potatoes

leek

ginger

cucumbers

mint

Fruit and vegetables (cont.)

variety of salad vegetables

variety of fresh fruits for snacks

banana (1)

lemons

Dairy and refrigerated items

skim milk

low-fat cottage cheese

reduced-fat ricotta cheese

small block reduced-fat cheese

parmesan cheese

baby bocconcini cheese

light cream cheese

Feelgood flavoured milk

Canola margarine

low-fat ice cream

yoghurt, low-fat, artificially sweetened

Yoplait no-fat yoghurt, banana and creamy honey

low-fat plain yoghurt

hummus dip

tzatziki dip

frozen spinach

frozen mixed berries

Breads, cereals, and pantry items

wholemeal, wholegrain or rye bread

wholewheat Mountain bread

Vitawheat crackers*

corn thins

rice crackers

brown rice*

basmati rice

wholemeal pasta*

couscous

wholemeal self-raising flour*

wholemeal plain flour*

cornflour

natural muesli

rolled oats

Uncle Toby's Plus Fibre Mix

Kellogg's All-Bran

Uncle Toby's Protein Plus or *Weight Watchers Muesli*

*Kellogg's Sultana Bran**

pepper*

curry powder

cumin*

dried chives

mixed herbs*

bay leaves*

peppercorns*

basil*

paprika

ground coriander*

Breads, cereals, and pantry items (cont.)

oregano

cinnamon*

ground cloves*

bi-carb soda*

balsamic vinegar*

chicken stock liquid

olive oil

low-fat evaporated milk

canned tomatoes

canned corn kernels

canned asparagus

unsweetened tomato juice

blackcurrant juice

tomato paste*

tomato pasta sauce

salsa

Splenda powder*

mixed nuts

Vegemite

sugar-free orange marmalade

air-popped popcorn

salad dressing, low-kilojoule, no-oil*

custard powder*

canned fruit in natural juice

strawberry diet jelly

low-fat flavoured tuna

tuna canned in brine

Breads, cereals, and pantry items (cont.)

dried dates

dried fruit

diet chocolate or caramel topping

chocolate bar (30g)

wine

Meat, poultry, seafood and eggs

lean beef mince (500g)

beef roast

steak (120g)

chicken breast fillets (750g)

lean bacon

sliced meat from deli section – chicken, roast beef, ham

fish

chicken bones

eggs

SHOPPING LIST TIPS

■ Amounts or serving sizes of the items you buy depend on how many people in your household eat these foods.

■ Some items listed include minimum quantities required for one person.

■ Many items without quantities are everyday items that you probably have already, or that you've purchased in a larger size than is needed in the menu plan.

■ Many of the recipes in the menu plans make more than one serve. Freeze the leftovers to enjoy later.

*Check if these ingredients are left over from your shopping in week 1.

facts & figures

Measures and temperatures

Please refer to the following conversion tables for metric and imperial conversions.

Dry measures

Metric	Imperial	Metric	Imperial
15g	½ oz	315g	10 oz
30g	1 oz	345g	11 oz
60g	2 oz	375g	12 oz (¾ lb)
90g	3 oz	410g	13 oz
125g	4 oz (¼ lb)	440g	14 oz
155g	5 oz	470g	15 oz
185g	6 oz	500g	16 oz (1 lb)
220g	7 oz	750g	24 oz (1½ lb)
250g	8 oz (½ lb)	1kg	32 oz (2 lb)
280g	9 oz		

Liquid measures

Metric	Imperial	Metric	Imperial
30ml	1 fluid oz	250ml (1 cup)	8 fluid oz
60ml	2 fluid oz	300ml	10 fluid oz (½ pint)
100ml	3 fluid oz	500ml	16 fluid oz
125ml	4 fluid oz	600ml	20 fluid oz (1 pint)
150ml	5 fluid oz (¼ pint, 1 gill)	1000ml (1 litre)	1¾ pints
190ml	6 fluid oz		

Oven temperatures

	C° (Celsius)	F° (Fahrenheit)	Gas mark
Very slow	120	250	1
Slow	150	300	2
Moderately slow	160	325	3
Moderate	180–190	350–375	4
Moderately hot	200–210	400–425	5
Hot	220–230	450–475	6
Very hot	240–250	500–525	7

1 calorie = 4.2 kilojoules

resources

USEFUL DEFINITIONS

'Bad' fats include saturated and trans fats. For good health, and particularly if you are concerned about your cholesterol, it is essential to reduce saturated and trans fats in your diet.

Cholesterol is a special fatty substance normally present in the blood. It plays an important role in many of the body's functions. The level present in the blood may vary between individuals, depending on variables such as hereditary factors and dietary intake.

chOOz to lOOz Program® is a weight loss and weight management program developed by the author, Caron Milham. It is available as a group, individual and correspondence (at home) program. For further details: www.milhamdietitians.com

Diabetes is a condition where there is too much sugar in the blood. This sugar is in the form of glucose, which comes from the food we eat – mainly carbohydrates (sugars and starch). Diabetics must aim to keep their blood glucose level (BGL) between 4–8 mmol/L with diet and exercise management, and in some cases, medication.

Exchanges are a measuring tool to quantify the amount of food that can be consumed in a particular 'food group'. For example, one exchange of bread is 300 kilojoules (70 calories) and is equivalent to 1 slice bread, 2 *Ryvita*, 1½ *Weet-Bix* or ⅓ cup cooked rice. See the Exchange list on page 171.

Fat is one of the three major components of food. The others are carbohydrate and protein. All foods are combinations of fat, protein and carbohydrate. There are also different types of fat. No food is completely one type of fat but foods are classified according to the main type of fat they contain.

Fibre is the part of vegetable food that is not digested by the body and is found in wholegrain breads, cereals, legumes, fruit and vegetables. Fibre adds bulk to your meals without adding extra kilojoules. There are two different types: soluble and insoluble. Both are necessary for good health.

Free vegetables refers to unrestricted vegetables, listed on page 174. They can be eaten in larger quantities to add bulk and fibre. They are ideal for weight loss/control because they are low in carbohydrates and kilojoules but high in essential nutrients.

Froiling means frying in a small amount of water.

Glycaemic Index (GI) is a ranking of carbohydrates in food according to their effect on blood glucose (sugar) levels after eating.

Classification of GI values
• Low GI – 55 or Less
• Moderate GI – 56 to 69
• High GI – 70 or more

To use GI effectively you must:
1 Compare carbohydrate foods of the same 'food group'.
2 Consider also the amount of fat, sugar and salt content.
3 Consider the valuable nutrients a food can contribute.
4 Look at your complete meal to see how this will affect your BGLs.

HDL cholesterol or high-density lipoprotein is one of the two major types of cholesterol. It is known as 'good cholesterol' because it takes cholesterol (LDL) to the liver to be broken down and excreted from the body.

'Healthy' fats are essential for good health and have been shown to protect against cancer and heart disease, as well as providing many health benefits. They include monounsaturated and polyunsaturated fats. Polyunsaturated fats can be further categorised to Omega-3 and Omega-6 types.

Hypertension (high blood pressure) is a risk factor for heart disease and stroke. Losing weight (if overweight) and reducing salt (sodium) intake, are important to assist with its management.

resources

Insoluble fibre helps keep your digestive system healthy and regular. It is found in higher amounts in wheat, rye and rice bran.

LDL cholesterol or low-density lipoproteins (LDL) is one of the two major types of blood cholesterol. It is known as 'bad cholesterol' because it can clog arteries when found in high concentrations. Having a high LDL is a major risk factor for heart disease.

Long-chain Omega-3s are the most beneficial Omega-3s and include EPA (eicosapentaenoic acid), DHA (docosahexaenoic acid) and DPA (docosapentaenoic acid). These are also called the 'marine Omega-3s', because fish and seafood are the richest sources of these nutrients.

Monounsaturated fats can help lower your total cholesterol levels if they replace some of the saturated and trans fats in your diet. They are found in monounsaturated oils including canola, olive and peanut oil, avocadoes, olives, nuts, seeds and lean meat.

Omega-3 fatty acids are one of the two types of polyunsaturated fats and include ALA (alpha-linolenic acid), EPA, DHA and DPA. They are found in oily fish, linseeds, walnuts, pecans, soybeans, canola oil and dark green vegetables. Omega-3s

assist with reducing total cholesterol levels and blood pressure and also have major roles in influencing growth and development, cardiovascular disease, brain development and function, diabetes and inflammatory diseases, including arthritis.

Omega-6 fatty acids are one of the two types of polyunsaturated fats. They help reduce your total cholesterol, LDL cholesterol and triglycerides. They are found in polyunsaturated oils and margarines, including sunflower, safflower, soy, grape seed, sesame and corn, nuts, seeds, wheat germ and legumes.

Saturated fats are fats that increase blood cholesterol levels, and are found in full-fat dairy products, fatty meats, butter, some margarines, coconut milk or cream, some vegetable oils (e.g. palm oil), and many commercial biscuits, cakes and pastries, snack foods and takeaways. They are solid at room temperature.

Salt (or sodium chloride) is the main source of sodium in our diet (it contains 40% sodium). Around 15% of the sodium in our diet comes from salt that we add and 75% from processed and commercially prepared food.

Soluble fibre slows the time it takes for food to pass through the digestive system resulting in

a slow, steady uptake of nutrients and reduced level of cholesterol absorption. It is found is in bread, some breakfast cereals (particularly oat-or barley-based), fruit, vegetables and legumes/beans.

Trans fats are made by transforming vegetable oils through a process called hydrogenation. They can increase blood levels of bad LDL cholesterol and decrease levels of good HDL cholesterol, and therefore increase your risk of heart disease. They are found in deep-fried fast foods and in pies, cakes and biscuits made with margarine and shortening.

Triglycerides (TGS) are a measure of the amount of fat circulating in the blood and are often measured at the same time as cholesterol levels. A high level of TGS can often lead to a low level of 'good' cholesterol (HDL) and increase the risk of heart disease.

USEFUL WEBSITES

Cancer Council Australia
www.cancer.org.au
Fact files on simple ways to reduce your cancer risk; information on early detection of cancer.

Caron Milham & Associates
www.milhamdietitians.com
Author Caron Milham's website features regularly updated nutrition and diet tips, weight-loss information and recipes.

Diabetes Australia
www.diabetesaustralia.com.au
Includes comprehensive information on diabetes guidelines, downloadable resources, newsletter, useful links and subsidised products.

Dietitians' Association of Australia (DAA)
www.daa.asn.au
Practical and up-to-date information on food and nutrition from Australia's largest professional nutrition organisation. Includes tips, recipes and contact details of Australian APDs.

Food Standards Australia New Zealand (FSANZ)
www.foodstandards.gov.au
Includes a Nutrition Panel Calculator to calculate the average nutrient content of food products.

Glycaemic Index
www.glycaemicindex.com
The official website of the glycaemic index. Includes an alphabetical table of carbohydrate foods, listing their GI per 100 g.

Go for 2 & 5
www.gofor2and5.com.au
Australian government health initiative website, recommending the benefits of having two fruit and five vegetables serves a day. Tips for how to increase your fruit and vegetable intake as well as quick and easy recipes.

Heart Foundation
www.heartfoundation.com.au
Information on risk factors and warning signs of heart attack and heart conditions, the latest research statistics, plus healthy food and exercise tips.

National Health and Medical Research Council, Australian Government
www.nhmrc.gov.au/publications/synopses/dietsyn.htm
Contains Nuturient Reference Values for Australia and New Zealand, including recommended daily intakes. Download the *Dietary guidelines for Australians* (PDF, Word, Zip).

USEFUL PUBLICATIONS

Australian Healthy Shopping Guide (1st edition) by Caron Milham. Starburst Publishing, 2007. Takes the guesswork and hard work out of making healthier choices in the supermarket. Helps you find products lower in sugar, fat, salt and kilojoules and those higher in fibre and nutrients. Companion to the *Australian Healthy Cooking Guide*.

Healthy Eating for Australian Families by Rosemary Stanton. Murdoch Books, 2007.

Nutrition for Life by Catherine Saxelby – 20th Anniversary Edition. Hardie Grant, 2006.

A Random House book
Published by Random House Australia Pty Ltd
Level 3, 100 Pacific Highway, North Sydney, NSW 2060
www.randomhouse.com.au

First published by Random House Australia in 2008

Copyright © Caron Milham 2008

Addresses for companies within the Random House Group can be found at
www.randomhouse.com.au/offices.

National Library of Australia
Cataloguing-in-Publication Entry

Milham, Caron.
The Australian healthy cooking guide.
ISBN: 978 1 74166 792 9 (pbk.)
Cookery.
641.563

Cover and internal design and typesetting by Voss Design
Printed and bound by Sing Cheong Printing Co. Ltd, Hong Kong
10 9 8 7 6 5 4 3 2 1